"Once, down a dark alleyway, a struggling TCK bumped into a mysterious Zen master, a grinning comedian, and an author of thrillers. That alleyway and these personas reside at O'Shaughnessy's center. He goes through countless cultural clashes, and the sum of his experience results in this book. His stories make the theory live, encourage you to follow your heart, and to avoid...

Douglas W Ota
Does to People
...ats Should Do About It
...passage.nl | www.dougota.nl

"I found Christopher's book to be very informative and easy to read. He does a marvelous job of covering the characteristics of the Third Culture Kid and makes them understandable with riveting examples taken from his own life as a TCK. Thanks for this valuable addition to the TCK literature and most importantly, the teen TCK."

Lois J Bushong, Licensed Marriage/Family Therapist, Author,
Belonging Everywhere and Nowhere: Insights into Counseling the Globally Mobile

"A much-welcomed addition to literature supporting TCKs/CCKs growing up in this increasingly global, mobile world. Christopher O'Shaughnessy skillfully approaches cross-cultural upbringings and transitions with insight, compassion and humorous tales of identity, connection, community, belonging and resilience."

Linda A Janssen, Author,
The Emotionally Resilient Expat: Engage, Adapt and Thrive Across Cultures

"I thought I was looking into a mirror, then I realized... It was a book! It's a very accurate and relatable description of TCKs."

Ryan Parker, TCK

"Through philosophical discourse and humorous personal anecdotes, Christopher O'Shaughnessy has created a thoroughly engaging, entertaining and informative book. Such an enjoyable literary style could only be achieved by a writer who grew up as a CCK and TCK. As I read through the chapters I felt a strong sense of Christopher's character and personality. Although already familiar with many of the works referenced in *Arrivals, Departures and the Adventures In-Between*, reading this insightful book has deepened my awareness and understanding of many issues and concepts surrounding TCKs. This is a must read for people involved in the education and development of TCKs. Every TCK should read it!"

Colin Walker, Director of Student Life
International School of Zug and Luzern Switzerland

"*Arrivals, Departures and the Adventures In-Between* is a TCK's guide to life! O'Shaughnessy's first book is an easy, energetic, and humorous read about life as a Third Culture Kid. It will keep your teenager engaged as Chris takes stories from his own life that kids can relate to, and gives them guidelines to take their stories and make them applicable in their own lives. You will look at a TCK's life in a more positive way as the book gives our kids meaning and purpose to the crazy and wonderful world of a TCK."

Jackie O'Farrell, mom of 2 TCK kids

"Christopher O'Shaughnessy's *Arrivals, Departures, and the Adventures In-Between* is a must read for high school-aged Third Culture Kids. And all of us who work with those kids who have grown-up in different cultures than their parents and ask, "Where am I from?" I have heard Christopher speak on the subject of TCKs numerous times and his use of humor and story-telling always connects him to his audiences, be they school-aged students or adult teaching staff and parents. I am pleased Christopher has stuck with what has worked well for him in the past. His keen sense of humor and ability to employ stories effectively has served him well and make this book readable and the important lessons easy to grasp. This is a great book about a very important topic in our rapidly changing and increasingly transient world."

Gary P Melton, Ed.D., Middle /High School Principal Mont'Kiara
International School, Kuala Lumpur, Malaysia

"Christopher O'Shaughnessy's book provides an honest and hilarious portrayal of the TCK lifestyle, including the worries and excitement, while giving support and understanding to all Third Culture Kids – I highly recommend this book."

Anna Foster, American TCK

"In *Arrivals, Departures, and the Adventures In-Between*, international speaker and TCK Christopher O'Shaughnessy provides a treasure trove of helpful information tucked within pages of true, personal stories.

Christopher writes like he talks – humorous and genuine. His book will benefit and bless most cross-cultural and third-culture students (and their parents/teachers) as he sheds light on topics such as making, keeping, and letting go of friends; conflict resolution and communication; restlessness, rootlessness, and preparing for the future; family, national identity, and grief.

Every TCK who is a junior or senior in high school should read this book prior to going off to college or life on their own. The concept of the way a TCK is wired being slightly ahead of the times – and leading the way in which our society is headed – provides new and challenging thoughts for TCKs and CCKs entering the work force in the coming years."

Delana H Stewart, Education Consultant, Author, *Nine Year Pregnancy*

"Christopher's book is a prime source of understanding for Third Culture Kids. His experiences give TCKs insight into their own backgrounds. Any TCK will relate to, and feel a connection with, his book and gain self understanding."

Luke Sweeney, International Student and TCK

"Christopher has managed to capture the essence of what it means to be a TCK and CCK. His book offers humorous stories giving light to the truths that TCKs and CCKs face as a result of their experiences. This book is a great read and offers practical tools and advice for those in the midst of being TCKs and CCKs. He has put into words many of the feelings and circumstances we have experienced as a family, and opened my eyes to the many positives we possess as a result of living internationally."

Lynn Kujawski, American expat and parent of a CCK

"This book is valuable life advice for TCKs and CCKs braided within witty stories. It also offers anyone who did not grow up globally mobile a walk-around in shoes that provide insight and understanding about the TCKs and CCKs in their lives."

Myra Dumapias, CEO of TCKid | Building Cross Cultural Bridges, www.TCKid.com

First Published in Great Britain 2014 by Summertime Publishing

© Copyright Christopher O'Shaughnessy

All rights reserved. No part of this publication may be reproduced, stored in, or introduced into a retrieval system, or transmitted, in any form, or by any means (electronic, mechanical, photocopying, recording or otherwise) without the prior written permission of the publisher.

This book is sold subject to the condition that it shall not, by way of trade or otherwise, be lent, resold, hired out, or otherwise circulated without the publisher's prior consent in any form of binding or cover other than that in which it is published and without a similar condition including this condition being imposed on the subsequent purchaser.

ISBN 978-1-909193-72-7

Cover design by Cornelia G. Murariu

Illustrations by Ruth 'Gunch' Dias,
www.diasphotography.com

Designed by Creationbooth.com

ARRIVALS
DEPARTURES
AND THE
ADVENTURES
IN-BETWEEN

CHRISTOPHER O'SHAUGHNESSY

ACKNOWLEDGEMENTS

First of all, I'd like to acknowledge the people who take the time to read the acknowledgements page. It's much harder to write than you might imagine, so thanks for being willing to appreciate this often overlooked part of a book.

It's taken the investment of many people for this book to come about. Among those who have contributed to the launch of this literary ship of dreams, I want to mention a few in particular.

Thanks to Mom for her unwavering support and steadfast love. Thanks to Dad for his constant encouragement and belief in me. Thanks to Gunch for the marvelous illustrations and for giggling with me until we're an incomprehensible spectacle of silliness. Thanks to Meg for being gentle and caring while simultaneously strong and radical.

I'm grateful to Heather Glass for motivating me to get this done!

To say this book would be possible without the immense contributions made to the world of TCKs and CCKs by Ruth Van Reken would be utter nonsense. From the foundational work, *Third Culture Kids: The Experience of Growing Up Among Worlds* (co-written by Ruth with David C. Pollock), to her continuing endeavors to love and serve those in global transition, Ruth has truly changed the world. She is nothing short of a legend and I am honored to be able to do what I do because of the trail she is still blazing. Thank you so much, Ruth.

To those who are mentioned in this book – my family, Auline (Karen) Platt, Luke Ware, Martin, Katka, Barry Walter, Colleen Jenkins, and everyone who was any part of the stories I've shared: thanks for being part of such teachable moments.

My dear Pups from the Faulty Flats, that amazing chapter of our lives did so much to shape who I am today. Truly and sincerely I cannot thank you enough for such an incredible experience.

For every generation of Teaology guys who have given of their precious free time to drink tea and discuss theology, sociology, and comedy with me: I am privileged. You were the testing ground for many of the ideas in this book.

So many students, parents, teachers, administrators, youth ministers, and counselors shared of their knowledge and experiences to make this happen. I couldn't have done this without you.

Caitlin Morse (my booking assistant), and Benjamin Cundy (my creative marketing guru): I am fortunate to have beloved and supportive friends who also happen to be talented colleagues.

Incredible thanks goes to Jo Parfitt and Jane Dean at Summertime Publishing for their guidance and hard work.

Many thanks also to Graham Booth for design services.

Finally, to my friends and loved ones across the globe for venturing with me, inspiring me, putting up with me, and supporting me: thanks for playing!

TABLE OF CONTENTS

FOREWORD:
Ruth E. Van Reken, co-author,
Third Culture Kids: Growing Up Among Worlds xi

PREFACE:
My Reasons For Writing This Book xv

USING THE 'QR' CODES xvii

CHAPTER 1
Being Foreign Where Foreigners Don't Belong..........1
Identity: Cross Cultural Kids and Third Culture Kids

CHAPTER 2
The Naked Truth about Relationships 31
Making friends, keeping friends, and letting go friends

CHAPTER 3
Don't Run... Use Your Words 59
Conflict resolution and communication

CHAPTER 4
Air Raid Sirens and Gangster Rap..............................81
Confidence in change

CHAPTER 5
Live in the Now, but Don't Get Kidnapped.............101
Restlessness, rootlessness, and preparing for the future

Chapter 6
Good Grief, Look at my British Teeth 123
Dealing with family, national identity, and grief

Chapter 7
Budget Airlines and Internet Cafés 147
Dealing with arrogance and building community

Chapter 8
Global Trends in Train Liberation 169
The world is catching up to the TCK experience, so what do we do?

Resources 191

About the Author 195

FOREWORD

Did you know that all over the world, young people like you are growing up very differently from how kids in the past grew up? People – maybe even your parents – grew up in places where most people not only spoke the same language, wore similar types of clothing and ate familiar foods, but also shared the same cultural traditions, saw life from a similar perspective and pretty much agreed on what things were right or wrong for a person or society to do.

Instead, many of you have grown up in communities where your friends and people around you speak all kinds of languages. Your outfits range from blue jeans and t-shirts to saris or chadors. Eating strange foods from all sorts of countries is an adventure rather than a fear. Practically every day it seems some friend is celebrating a religious or cultural holiday you never heard about before you met that friend. Rather than living in a world where most adults in the community reflect the values taught in your school, some of you may find yourselves living under different rules or expectations at home from what you learn at school. And if your grandparents are from different countries or cultures, you find going back and forth between them changes the language you have to speak or the way you greet them and so forth.

So what's the 'matter' with growing up like this? After all, you get to see the world close up – even if you don't travel a lot, the world has come to you. It's really interesting to get to know people from so many places and cultures. Why is Christopher writing a book for us?

Well, you're right. Nothing at all is the 'matter' for those who, like me, like Christopher, like you, grow up in this kind of rich diversity. For me, it is one of the greatest gifts of my life that I grew up as an American child in Kano, Nigeria. I learned so much by having friends from many different countries and cultures. I loved it all.

But there was something I didn't realize was happening. As I adjusted my behavior and language depending on who I was with, I was starting to live in a neither/nor world. In Nigeria, I assumed places where I seemed different from the local people were simply because I was a US American. It was okay to be different because that's what others and I, myself, expected. But when I returned to the USA at age 13, I suddenly found myself feeling very different in the place I always thought I was 'from'. So now what? I wasn't quite Nigerian enough, but it didn't seem like I was quite US American enough either.

And that's the new deal. When most folks grew up in pretty much one place where everyone around them was pretty much alike too, it wasn't so hard to figure out "Who am I?" Part of finding a sense of belonging somewhere is learning how the people in this place do things by what our parents, relatives, teachers, media, and peers teach us as we interact with them. People used to learn these rules as children, maybe tested them while they were teens, but then kind of took them in as their own and moved out into adulthood with a pretty clear sense of who they were and where they belonged.

But what happens when you keep switching between worlds where the rules might be quite different? (Just think what happens to a driver who doesn't understand that the rule for driving in this new place is to drive on the left instead of the right like he used to do!) You may be learning a terrific skill set useful in today's world – how to relate to different cultures and people, even to be a cultural bridge. But how do you figure out which of these many worlds you have experienced is the one you can claim as your own? Or say you are 'from'? If you have to pick just one, then what about the rest of you?

Well, that's why you're going to enjoy reading this book. Christopher has been there/done that. He's lived all over the world and he understands. Plus, he's got a lot of great and funny stories. I enjoyed reading the book and know it's going to help so many growing up in this new way to begin to put the pieces of their own stories together – in good ways so that you not only understand yourself better, but can also use the things you learned while living this life among and between so many different kinds of world. I'm really glad Christopher has taken the time to share his story with you.

Hope you enjoy your own life journey as much as I have my own once I began to understand how the many different pieces of my life fit together. I wish this book had been written when I was younger.

Ruth E. Van Reken
Co-author, *Third Culture Kids:*
Growing Up Among Worlds

PREFACE

Well, hello and welcome! Thanks for joining me. I usually work as a public speaker and am spoiled because most audiences, out of politeness, applaud at the beginning of a presentation – before I've done anything. I know it's unorthodox, but it would make me feel much better if you'd apply the same tradition of politeness to reading this book. That's right, please applaud now for the pages you're about to read. Of course, I'll never know if you've actually clapped. That's one of the difficulties in writing versus giving a live presentation. Still, I feel it's been well worth writing this book to complement what I do as a speaker.

I've been fortunate to work with kids and young adults who've grown up moving around the world, or living in the highly transient international environment, for about 15 years. In that time I've come to appreciate first hand how powerful it is to find a sense of belonging and purpose. Those who grow up in transit between different cultures often have a harder time finding the words and concepts to express who they are and discover where they belong. All too often they end up comparing themselves – inaccurately and unfairly – to more anchored or established groups, and in doing so feeling alone, abnormal, or worse. Or they miss out on opportunities to contribute all they have to offer because they don't appreciate the incredible gifts they possess as a result of of their cross-cultural upbringing.

Through this book, my hope is to open a door to understanding who we are as people who grow up among worlds. I'll strive to help make sense of the challenges we face and capabilities we have as a result, and maybe even spark some inspiration to make a difference in a world moving closer and closer to our own experience every day. Part of knowing who you are is believing you've got something to give – and to know you've got something to give, you've got to believe in who you are.

It's exciting times, so... on with the book!

USING THE 'QR' CODES

You'll notice little 'QR' codes ('quick response' advanced barcodes) throughout the book. Using a QR code reader app on your smart phone (look for free QR code reader apps in your app store) you can scan these codes to launch additional content – bonus material, one might say – to go along with this book.

Go on, give it a try – it makes things more interactive!

XI

CHAPTER 1

BEING FOREIGN WHERE FOREIGNERS DON'T BELONG

IDENTITY: CROSS CULTURAL KIDS AND THIRD CULTURE KIDS

I was a robot. At least I firmly believed I was when I was a child. And I don't mean in an emotionally cold or lack of feeling sort of way. No, I really thought I was a mechanical creation put together with circuits, wires, chips, batteries, and hopefully some laser cannons I just hadn't discovered yet. I reached this conclusion late one night in my early childhood. I was living in the small village of Fressingfield nestled deep in the English countryside, and my imagination was as vast as the fields that surrounded our quaint bungalow on a pig farm.

As my parents tucked me into bed on a cold winter night, I tried to slow my racing mind and fall asleep. Being a six-year-old boy with an overactive imagination, falling asleep wasn't always quick or easy. Clad in pajamas, I tossed and turned, hoping to find the ideal position to lull my body to rest. After a minute or two, I decided I was too hot and flung the covers away. But then I decided I was too cold, and drew the covers back over me. As I did, I saw a sparkle in the darkness between my sheets. It was nothing more than a quick shimmer, but it was enough to startle me and pique my curiosity. What on earth was something sparkly doing in my bed?

I lay in silence, slightly scared but incredibly curious, hoping it would come back. Whatever it was, it was invisible now – perhaps I'd scared it away. I held my breath motionless, straining to see in the darkness, wishing it to return and twinkle again. After what seemed like an eternity (but was more likely less than a minute), I accepted that the magic (or whatever it was) had gone. Perhaps it had just been a figment of my imagination. Imaginary figments did leak out of my mind from time to time. No longer straining to be still, I drew the covers back over me. The sparks returned! There was no doubt in my mind: I had definitely seen a burst of what looked like electricity when I moved.

I repeated the motion I'd just made and was astounded to see that I had caused the sparks again – right on my knees where they had rubbed against the sheets! My knees could produce electrical sparks! In light of such irrefutable evidence, what conclusion could I draw except that I must be a robot? My mind was spinning. How had my parents fooled me for so long? Were my two sisters robots as well? Were my parents robots? Was EVERYONE a robot? Did adults perpetuate the myth of being alive like a fairytale? Then things started to get out of hand. Why were my knees sparking? They'd never done that before. Was I broken? Was I going to short circuit... or DIE? Could I die? Should I be rebooted? I was working myself into a panic and I had to have answers IMMEDIATELY!

"MOM! DAD! Come quickly!" I yelled from the darkness of my room. My voice conveyed the panic I was feeling as it echoed down the hall. Dutifully (and with a clear sense of concern mixed with exhaustion), my parents hurried to my room. As they opened the door, I assaulted them with a burst of what must have been utterly incomprehensible accusations, questions, and wild explosions of indignation. How could they not have told me? Were there replacement parts hidden somewhere in the house? Would they please get me some new knees? Was I combustible?

My parents listened – perplexed – as I spouted off my concerns. My mother leaned in to check the temperature of my forehead. Wise, I thought. I bet my processor is going to overheat as I evaluate all of this. Finally, when I had slowed down enough for my parents to get a few words in, they asked if I was feeling ill. I shot back with anger this time. No, I wasn't feeling ill! How could they even dare keep up the act now that I knew the truth?

"The truth about what?" my father asked.

"The truth about me being a robot." I responded confidently, waiting for their faces to drop and the obligatory, "Oh, we knew we'd have to tell you someday..." conversation to begin.

Instead, my revelation was met with blank stares. So I proceeded to explain how I'd seen sparks coming out of my knees: clear evidence that I was, in fact, a mechanical being powered by some form of electricity. I demanded they give me the whole story, being careful not to leave out which weapons came preinstalled and what sort of options were available for future add-ons if I promised to save up enough money to pay for them myself.

What followed was my parents' attempt at explaining static electricity to me. It took a while because I was quite convinced of my newly discovered robotic identity. Finally, it began to sink in that I was not a mechanical being. I had no hidden laser cannons and I could not be upgraded to run faster or fly.

As silly as it sounds, this bizarre little escapade left me feeling rather sad for a while. The whole thing may have been the product of a ridiculously overactive imagination, but it touched on an issue central to our human existence – identity. I may have been young, but for a short while I was tantalizingly close to having what I thought was an exciting distinctiveness in the world. When those hopes were dashed, I wallowed in an oddly powerful feeling of disappointment. I was just normal, nothing special.

Identity

Identity is a funny and complicated thing. Certainly most of us have, at some point, yearned to be extraordinary, unique, and special. But we've probably also longed to fit in, be normal, and stay safely unremarkable, as well. In my life, far more examples of this type of issue come to mind – most of which have been far more painful than finding out I'm not a robot.

Several years after learning about static electricity, my world was turned upside down when my father announced that we were moving to the United States. Dad worked for the U.S. Air Force, and my family's military heritage went back several generations. My father was born on a U.S. military base in Germany and spent part of his childhood on installations in France; my grandfather had fought in and survived the Korean War. I had been born in the U.K. as was my youngest sister, Meg, six years later – and we had moved to the U.S. and back once already (though I was too young to remember). In fact, my other sister, Gunch (not the name given to her by my parents, but the name that younger me decided she should have and imposed upon her – quite successfully), was born two years after me in the U.S.

While living in England, we rarely visited the air base where my father worked. For the most part we lived far enough away that we were not heavily influenced by military or American culture. My parents' decision to live on a pig farm may have been born out of necessity (there wasn't much affordable housing closer to the airbase at the time), but we thoroughly enjoyed local village life – I had barely any sense that I was at all different from my fellow British friends.

Having received Uncle Sam's marching orders, we prepared to resettle across the pond. I remember being very excited to move. In my young mind the United States of America was big, flashy, exciting, and a million years more advanced than the sleepy English village I had called home for as much of my short life as I could remember.

The military had need of my father's services at Nellis Air Force base in Las Vegas, Nevada, a place drastically different from Fressingfield, England. It was hot. It was bright. It was loud. It was full of people, not livestock. I had lived in a bungalow on a pig farm in England. In comparison our new house, located in a sprawling suburb of a vast city of endless entertainment, was infinitely more spacious and seemed like a mansion. In place of a front garden with grass and rose bushes, we had several artistically arranged piles of pebbles: a rock garden. This was the most absurd and amusing thing to me, but does make sense in the middle of a desert, I suppose.

Looking back, I feel not a day went by in the first year I lived in Las Vegas that I wasn't stunned, startled, or amused by some new detail of life there. In England, a mere three and a half TV channels played on our tiny black-and-white television: the faithful BBC 1 and 2, ITV, and sound but no picture from Channel 4. In Las Vegas, friends in my neighborhood were privy to channel selections that numbered in the hundreds – and all in color!

Nothing, however, better showcased how different my new life in Las Vegas was than going to school. Back in Fressingfield, I'd attended a primary school with close to 100 students up to the equivalent of fifth grade. It was an old-fashioned school. 'Dinner ladies' cooked us real meals and served them on real plates with real cutlery. Manners were of the utmost importance, and it was perfectly acceptable for a teacher, dinner lady, or any other authority figure to deliver a swift and decisive smack to the backside of any wily child not adhering to the customs and courtesies being diligently instilled in us.

Now here I was in Las Vegas, a nervous seven-year-old standing in the enormous shadow of my new elementary school. It housed more than ten times the number of students enrolled in my previous school. The actual building appeared to have been built out of a giant discarded Tetris block. It was a massive grey concrete cube periodically dotted with peach-colored doors that contained the only windows to be found on the entire edifice. The air around the building shimmered with heat as the sun baked the asphalt and gave the whole scene an otherworldly appearance.

Nestled deep inside this enormous cube was my second grade classroom. Being led there on my first day, I was sure I would never remember which set of identical peach doors to enter, nor which complicated combination of turns would bring me to my assigned educational chamber. One of the first things I noticed was what a backwards sensation it was to come indoors here: the outside was scorching hot and inside was chilly thanks to the powerful air conditioners that were a necessity in nearly every building in Las Vegas. Rarely did summers in the U.K. get to a point where one would need to cool a building by any means more powerful than opening a window.

As I entered my classroom, I was greeted with a sight that caused my heart to stop momentarily and panic to overtake me. The room was filled with the loud chatter of several dozen children. Kids were running, screaming, yelling, and causing general mayhem. Two boys were being taped to the wall, and something appeared to be on fire in the corner of the room. It was so chaotic! This wild frenzy of noise and activity was a far cry from what I expected to find in a classroom. In Fressingfield, students sat quietly in anticipation of a teacher's arrival. When a teacher (or any adult) entered the room, every student would quickly stand in silence behind their chair waiting for the signal to be seated. If a teacher arrived to find loud chattering or (almost unimaginably) children running around, it was grounds for execution... or so we believed.

Now, as I stood amidst mayhem that would have warranted unspeakable punishment in the world I came from, I was frozen with fear. I wanted nothing to do with the madness I had been thrust into. I wanted

Being Foreign Where Foreigners Don't Belong

to remain alive and wanted desperately not to be around when a teacher arrived and began annihilating these reckless children. As I considering running out of the door I had just entered, I watched in amazement as an adult who definitely carried herself like a teacher entered the room. As if completely oblivious to the uproar all around her, she quietly made her way to a desk and began scribbling notes on a piece of paper. Perhaps she was studying the list of pupils she would soon condemn to death and in which order they would receive their well-deserved fates.

Just then, a loud synthesized gong boomed from an intercom system perched just above the door. Like magic, the room froze. By the sound of the second gong, you could have almost heard a pin drop. The fire was extinguished and the children who had been taped to the wall were miraculously free. Simultaneously, the entire class stood and faced the American flag hoisted in the corner of the room. They then raised their right hands and placed them over their hearts. Just when I didn't think it could get any stranger, the whole class, in unison, began to recite what I would later learn was The Pledge of Allegiance.

Not wanting to look out of place, I hastily adopted the same stance as everyone else. Unfortunately, I happen to be left-handed and so instinctively covered my heart with my left hand (which, I later found out, is considered unacceptable) and listened to the voices reciting patriotic poetry all around me. The only patriotic thing I knew was *God Save the Queen*, and so, not wanting to be the only one standing in silence, I began to recite the U.K.'s national anthem.

It wasn't only the words coming out of my mouth that betrayed how unique I was compared to those around me. Having come from an island usually covered in cloud, I was markedly paler than anyone else in the classroom. I was also dressed about a decade behind everyone else. My fellow students wore baggy, neon-colored t-shirts and knee-length shorts. I was inadvertently blinding the class with the light reflecting from the vast swathes of pasty leg my incredibly short navy-blue shorts revealed. My forest-green shirt was tight around my chest as was the fashion in the U.K. at the time. You could easily have made three of my shirts from the material of just one of the baggy garments my classmates sported. There I stood: an oddly dressed, starkly pale, timid boy clutching his heart with his (unintentionally disrespectful) left hand, reciting (again, unintentionally disrespectful) words of allegiance to the very crown and monarchy from which the country whose flag I stood before had fought to free itself from.

Sadly, The Pledge of Allegiance is not a terribly long work, and, as I had started late, I was not able to finish my one-man homage to the Queen before the rest of the students finished their patriotic recital. In the silence that followed their morning routine, one small voice could be heard uttering the final lines to *God Save the Queen* in a thick British accent. "Send her victorious, happy and glorious, long to reign over us. God save the Queen." All eyes fixed on me. Gasps took in so much air that the oxygen in the room may have become scarce. But thin air was not enough to save me from the impending wrath of Mrs. Bower.

While she had seemed strangely calm amidst the chaos of the classroom initially, Mrs. Bower was alarmingly agitated in the stillness in which I now seemed to be held captive. What followed was a stern lecture about the importance of patriotism and severe warnings that antics of the magnitude I had just displayed would not be tolerated. She continued at high decibels in front of an audience of stunned and somewhat bemused students. For my part, I could not figure out what I had done wrong. But I was sure that whatever unknown infraction I had committed I could well be executed for it I tried it again.

Fitting In

This was the beginning of my ongoing struggle to fit in. I didn't want to be a spectacle. I didn't want to upset people and not know why. I didn't want to be an oddity who sparked people's curiosity but didn't engender their friendship. Unfortunately, my accent drew quite a bit of attention on the playground. Kids found the way I pronounced things to be a never-ending source of amusement. I would be bombarded daily by requests to repeat words. Simple words like 'water' became the bane of my existence. While 'water' is spelled with a 't' in the middle, most Americans pronounce it with a 'd.' That I used a 't' sound was nothing short of magical to my fellow classmates. It didn't take long before I decided to purposefully put an end to the accent I had unknowingly acquired in England.

For much of my first year of school in Las Vegas, I was unnaturally quiet. I didn't speak to anyone beyond my few friends in anything more than a whisper, and even then, only if truly necessary. At meetings with my teacher, my parents were always shocked to hear that I was such a remarkably quiet boy. I certainly wasn't at home. But at school I was very quiet because I was listening. I was desperately trying to gauge and emulate the nuances of an American accent. To further my research, I watched as much television as I could. I'm living proof that TV is a marvelously effective way to learn an accent. After just a year, I had mastered American pronunciation.

I worked hard to blend in, to be accepted as normal rather than scrutinized as an oddity. At this young stage in life, I learned to be a chameleon. Four years after arriving in Las Vegas, Uncle Sam deposited us back across the pond in the U.K. We relocated to a different area than the one in which we had previously lived, but the U.K. was still very familiar. Would I switch back to being 'British,' unlearning all the 'American-ness' I had worked so hard to master? Was this what people did? Continuously reinvent themselves each time their surroundings changed? That wasn't always possible. An accent can be altered, but what about unchangeable features like appearance or ethnicity? Everybody experiences change, but to have to continually adapt to a different environment made me feel a bit unstable. It seemed like a lot of work to make each place feel like home and to make myself feel relevant and accepted in each.

Looking back, I realize I was beginning to wrestle with the issue of identity. I was trying to define myself in the context of my surroundings. Who was I in the U.S. and who was I in the U.K.? Who would I be in the other places I would live? I had different friends, different surroundings, and even different dialects for the U.S. and U.K. Just by going between two somewhat similar countries I had developed multiple personalities. Imagine what people who move between more disparate countries must go through. I think everybody struggles at some point or another with their identity. How do we explain ourselves to ourselves and to other people?

Throughout my life I've found the simple question, "Where are you from?" to be a perfect example of how difficult it can be to explain myself to other people. Is it a question of where I was born or where I feel most at home? Where I am currently living or where I've lived the longest? Where I have citizenship? People have no idea what they are in for, or what difficulty they are causing by asking such a simple, yet loaded, question. At times, Americans have accused me of pretending to be British. While at university in the U.K. I remember giving in to the repeated pleas of my classmates to demonstrate my American accent for them. When I finally did, they didn't think it was very convincing and thought I was exaggerating my U.S. connections to seem cool. I felt like no matter which nationality I claimed to explain myself, it wasn't entirely true or accurate.

Eventually I learned to flagrantly lie in response to the exhausting question of origins. I told Americans I was from Chicago (I fly through there a lot, so I thought it should count), I told Brits I was from the Outer Hebrides (a set of sparsely populated islands northwest of Scotland – nobody questioned that), and if I really couldn't be bothered, I just responded in incomprehensible gibberish and strange noises. If you make peculiar enough sounds for long enough, nobody asks follow-up questions and you are off the hook with no further explanation needed. I've since learned simpler answers are better: *'You should be able to give someone all the information they need to know within ten seconds. If they're truly interested in the rest of your story, they'll ask. If not, why waste more time explaining yourself?'*[1]

So, odd noises aside, what does define us? What describes us? Is it our beliefs, customs, and the way we think and behave? Is it our language, likes, tastes, passions, and talents? Is it our history, nationality, worldview, and surroundings? Probably. That's what makes identity such an endeavor to figure out. It's messy, complicated and ultimately quite beautiful.

Helpful acronyms: Am I a CCK or TCK?

Many years, several countries, and a few moves later, I would learn the term Cross Cultural Kid (CCK) and realize the type of person they were describing was me. In the amazingly insightful book, *Third Culture Kids: Growing Up Among Worlds*, Ruth Van Reken explains that a CCK is pretty much just what it sounds like: someone who's grown up living in or interacting with different cultures[2]. Language, beliefs, traditions, values and social expectations are all aspects that form 'culture', which helps shape the way we make sense of the world around us. *'One is not born into a culture; they cultivate it through their years of living and experiencing.*'[3] In our changing world plenty of young people are interacting with significantly different cultural worlds as they grow up. As a result, there are plenty of ways someone could be a CCK: an immigrant or refugee child, someone who moved around a lot while growing up, someone who grows up as a racial or ethnic minority where they live – to name just a few. For someone growing up with parents from two very different cultural backgrounds, each time they visit their different grandparents, for example, what and how they eat, or the language they speak, may be quite distinct. All over the world, many local children now attend international schools where the culture and language they operate in during the day is a far cry from how they live once they return home each evening.

All this variety has led to the fact that there are several types of CCK – each with some distinct traits, but all sharing a lot of characteristics in common. I found out that I fall into a sub-category called Third Culture Kids (TCKs). The term TCK was coined by Dr Ruth Hill Useem in the 1950s. Clever people have been studying TCKs ever since, and the current and most widely accepted definition comes from David C. Pollock. In the broadest sense, a TCK is someone who has grown up in a culture (or cultures) different from their parents' culture (or cultures) and in many cases while experiencing frequent transitions. Dave explains that TCKs often relate to all the cultures they've experienced, but don't belong entirely to any one of them.[2] Usually, parents of TCKs plan on returning to their culture or country of origin, so TCKs tend to grow up in temporary stages, or amidst other peoples' temporary stages. Military brats, missionary kids, and people whose parents move their family because of their job form part of the TCK crowd.

Nowadays, a lot of people learn to operate in multiple cultures, and having to do so with a lack of stability, constantly relearning social structures amidst frequent changes during developmental years is part of the life-story of many TCKs. The reason it's called a 'third' culture doesn't have anything to do with the number of countries or cultures a person has lived in, and it's not just a mix created by other cultures; it has to do with the experience of growing up in-between cultures. For example, a first culture (although people can have several first cultures) has to do with a person's origins; usually where a person's parents are from and the passport(s) they hold. A second culture (although again, people can have several second cultures) is the environment a person has lived or is living in outside the parents' culture or cultures. The third culture is what's shared by people who live amidst first and second cultures. *'The third culture itself is a distinct way of life'*[4] different from either the first or second cultures. It's the third culture that means someone born in Argentina, living in Canada, and moving to Japan can relate to someone born in India, living in Switzerland, and moving to Australia. Their first and second cultures may be vastly different, but the third culture of being 'in-between' is familiar.[5]

I picture the third culture as being like a hallway that connects various rooms in a large building. Inside of each room is a distinct culture. When someone enters a room, they're immersed in that culture. For me, one room is American: I am a U.S. citizen with a passport to prove it. Another room is British: I've lived in the U.K. longer than anywhere else. Another room is the military: I was around it from the time I was born until I was an adult. And so on. I have moved, and still am moving between those and other various rooms. I get from room to room using a hallway that connects them. And in that hallway are loads of other TCKs (and CCKs) moving about between the rooms that make up their cultural story. It's comforting to know I'm not alone in the hallway and it feels good to be able to give knowing glances to, and get knowing glances from, others who know what it's like to move in and out of various rooms even if they're not the same rooms I frequent.

As a type of CCK, TCKs share a lot in common with other people whose life stories have been woven amidst different cultures. I'm writing from my experience growing up as a TCK and being fortunate enough to continue learning from, living around, and working with other TCKs. Because some very clever people have been studying TCKs in particular for a while, there's some good information already available to give insight to the experience – and much of it is transferable between TCKs and other types of CCKs. Ruth Van Reken says, *'studying TCKs is like a 'petri dish' – a place where we can see the effects of a cross-cultural childhood and mobility so common in today's world in their most basic form.'*[4] So, no matter what type of CCK you are, come along for the ride and find the parts of the adventure of living between the worlds you know that speak to you. It's an important ride to take because it delves into identity; and we all have to explore identity if we are going to be able to understand what an important role TCKs and other CCKs can play in society. For anyone to impact the world, they must first navigate their own individuality, but those who grow up traversing different cultural worlds often lack the language to undertake such an exploration. Sometimes *'...people who don't know and understand the terms 'third culture kid'... feel very much alone. They know they are different but cannot understand why. They think they are the only ones who feel this way and it must mean that there is something wrong with them.'*[6] In learning that I was a type of CCK, I also learned I was not alone. To me, understanding that I am a type of CCK like so many others of similar experience, makes far more sense than trying to explain I'm not quite any number of other things. *'Lacking an identity isn't something anyone can just 'get over.'*[7]

INVISIBLE ALIEN

Before I learned these terms, I really did think there was something wrong with me, as I had no way of explaining why I was *not quite* like others, even when I thought I should be. For example, I remember going to live in the U.S. immediately after attending an American military high school in the U.K. (before I started university) and being shocked at how foreign and out of place I felt. Not to mention how inexplicably difficult it was to explain myself.

I had spent all four years of high school around Americans (not actually in America, but on U.S. military bases overseas). I had mastered an American accent and felt pretty proficient in what I believed to be U.S. culture. But, as I would soon find out, life overseas (even if around other Americans) was not a substitute for life in the United States. Over the years, I've met countless people who grew up outside their country of citizenship or official origin, and time and again they shared that moving to the place they supposedly came from was far harder than a move to any foreign country.[8]

It can be a humbling experience. That may sound odd, but the reality is that living as a foreigner makes you different – special even. You stand out, perhaps not always in a good way, but you do have distinction.[9] Growing up on military bases, I could go inside compounds protected by armed guards and barbed wire as a matter of daily life, whereas the vast majority of the population could only peek through the fence. People who are part of the international community often enjoy special privileges through companies, organizations, or governments that the average person does not.[2]

When I arrived in the U.S., I looked and sounded like everyone else. No one could tell how different I actually was just by looking at me. One plane ride and I had become average and normal by all outside appearances. Looking back, it was more of a blow to my ego than I really liked to admit. I had been used to being 'special.' As one TCK who spent time in Central America puts it, *'I feel most comfortable being*

'The American' (but you can't be specially labeled that when you are already IN America). As a foreigner, I am automatically interesting (especially in Nicaragua, EVERYONE wants to know who I am and what I am about). When I landed in Denver, though, suddenly NOBODY CARED why I was here, no one stared at me, called me gringa *or* chelita, *no one chose to start conversations with me, because I just look like everyone else (and probably because no one cares, in an American airport, who you are and why you are there, they see travelers every day). I never thought of the possibility that I may miss being stared and gawked at all the time.'*[3]

Far worse than bruising my ego, looking and sounding like everyone around me proved to be disastrous. It masked the fact that I was totally unaware of many facets of life in the U.S. *'Being a foreigner in a foreign country is easy, you are seen as one so it's normal to feel like one. But upon entering the country of your birth or your familial origins, you realize that the place you are meant to feel the most 'at home' is the most foreign to you.'*[3] I'd missed famous commercials, had a different sense of fashion, and was lacking key elements of language like popular slang. I may have spoken with the correct accent, but much of my vocabulary was shaped by the military – I was proficient in a myriad of acronyms that suddenly meant absolutely nothing to those around me in the civilian world.

I had several embarrassing incidents where I simply did not understand the routine for things. Trying to get a driver's license in the U.S. was a huge debacle. For one thing, most people in the U.S. get their licenses at 16, which was preposterously young by the standards of most places I'd lived. As a result, I was a 'late bloomer' in the world of vehicular control. I was only really applying for a driver's license because I had quickly learned that it was the *de facto* form of identification in the U.S. I needed to get a driver's license so I could get a place to live. Ironically, it's very hard to get a license without first having a place to live. I was still staying with friends temporarily and the less-than-cordial, disgruntled employee at the DMV (Department of Motor Vehicles) – who had clearly been working there since Mr. Ford's marvelous driving contraptions first hit the streets and created the need for licenses, as well as the angry people who issue them – was less than amused with my attempts to squeeze my parents' U.K. address onto his official form. In a panic, I made up an address: 1615 West 14th Avenue. This apparently sounded legitimate enough to allow me to take to the streets with a driving instructor for a test.

I had actually taken quite a few driving lessons back in the U.K. and was very confident in the sound tutelage I had been given – with the obvious exception of which side of the road to drive on. As I sat in the car next to a rather uninterested testing official, I concentrated with all my might on staying on the right side of the road. I did fairly well at intersections, yielding, and even parallel parking. It was quite easy to remember which side of the road to stay on when there was other traffic around. Toward the end of the test the examiner had me drive through an industrial area with very wide streets and virtually no other vehicles. Probably because I was congratulating myself prematurely, and because there were no other cars to remind me, I instinctively drifted to the left. The instructor was filling out forms on his lap and didn't even notice. No one did – until I started driving directly into the path of an oncoming truck. The truck flashed his lights at me and let out an alarmingly prolonged blast from his horn to show he was neither amused at my being in his path, nor would he back down from this unintentional game of chicken. He clearly had the dominant vehicle.

Amazingly, my instructor still had his nose buried in forms. Rather than panic and jolt the steering wheel abruptly to return me to my rightful lane, I gently corrected my path and as subtly as possible, made my way back. Thinking I was just being a jerk, the oncoming truck continued his horn blast as we narrowly passed each other. Disturbed by the noise, my instructor looked up in time to have missed my *faux pas* and, glancing at the truck now barreling off behind us, commented that I would have to be aware of other discourteous drivers on the roads who loved to lay on the horn just to be obnoxious. That very afternoon, flying in the face of preparedness, I was deemed fit to operate a motor vehicle. Fortunately, during my relatively short stay in the U.S., I did not drive on a regular basis – I simply needed an ID.

Trying to go local

Even armed with a locally-issued ID, I still didn't feel local. My attempts to explain why I didn't understand what everyone around me took for granted were met with irritation and confusion. Strangely, it was at a fast-food restaurant that I finally unlocked the key to survival. I needed to try Mexican food, and so found a burrito-selling bistro and decided to dive in. It was the lunchtime rush and the poor over-worked cashier behind the counter didn't have the time or the patience to deal with my lack of knowledge regarding Mexican food terms. The menu before me was an exciting list of unknown and untested words; I wanted to choose wisely but had no idea how to do so. The crowd behind me was becoming anxious – violent even – and the fast-food worker in front of me was growing exasperated. Something inside me tripped back to a very hard-wired reaction from the British side of my upbringing. I reverted to my English accent and stammered out a detailed and heartfelt apology. "I'm terribly sorry. I'm quite unfamiliar with this type of cuisine. If you'd be so kind as to recommend what most people enjoy, I'll gladly take it and move along. I really am awfully sorry, it is my fault entirely. I promise I shall never again stall the finely-tuned food purveyance system your respectable establishment clearly had in operation before I so foolishly turned the whole thing pear-shaped."

No sooner had the words flopped apologetically out of my mouth than the whole atmosphere of the situation changed. I had unwittingly unleashed the power of the English accent in the U.S. People were no longer angry, they were charmed. Grimaces turned to smiles and exasperation gave way to sympathy. I was even given my meal for free with a surprisingly cheerful, "It's on the house, welcome to America!"

I sat down in a now very different, very friendly, crowded restaurant and enjoyed a marvelous burrito. This little trick would serve me well, but I couldn't help but feel I was a fraud. Yes, I had grown up in Britain and was, therefore, a visitor, due the patience and understanding that a foreigner with a notoriously charming accent should receive in a country of generally friendly people. But I was also technically an American, with an American accent and passport, who had grown up around Americans. I was a foreign countryman, a native outsider. I was a mess.

In practice, and despite what most people told me, I really was a foreigner. It was far easier for me to navigate my surroundings when I looked at my situation the same way I looked at other foreign places I had been. In her book, *The Global Nomad's Guide to University Transition,* Tina Quick wisely advises that, *'It is necessary to treat your home country the way you would any other foreign country because it is foreign to you in many ways.'*[6] In hindsight, understanding I was a TCK may not have stopped me from using my English accent to smooth things over, but I would have had the vocabulary to explain my situation. More than that, I would have understood why I was feeling the way I did. Knowing there was a name for what I was going through would have provided an anchor for my cultural transition, just as national identity might be an anchor for a long-term immigrant or even refugee. I could have devoted far more time and attention to adapting to my surroundings and taking in the culture around me.

But at the time, I wasn't armed with self-understanding, terminology, or language. And so, after just six months in my 'homeland,' I left. It was too hard feeling foreign in what I was told was my native land. I felt more comfortable being foreign where foreigners belonged… in foreign lands.

TO LABEL OR NOT TO LABEL? YES.

TCKs can react to finding out about the TCK experience in a variety of different ways. Generally, it ranges from "I don't think so, you can't label me," to "Thank goodness there's a name for who I am and what I'm experiencing!" I personally moved along the spectrum of those reactions from one end to the other.

I was first introduced to the term 'TCK' at a conference during my first year of university in the U.K. Working as an intern for a youth ministry organization, I was at a staff training meeting in Germany and an expert on TCKs had been brought in to teach on the subject. As she spoke, I felt more and more uncomfortable. She was describing experiences, moods, tendencies, and feelings that I had growing up and was actually still having. It was like she was inside my head. I didn't relate completely to *everything* she said, but enough of it was relevant to make me feel singled out and vulnerable. How could I be so predictable that a woman I had never met could describe parts of me when I didn't even have words for myself?

During a break in the session, I moved to a table in the back of the room. I couldn't escape the conference without drawing attention to myself, but I at least wanted some space between me and this psychic woman. Feeling a bit safer in the back, I waited for the speaker to continue her invasive presentation. She went on sharing pieces of my life without mentioning specifics. It was eerie and I felt angry at myself for being so formulaic. It was as if my originality was being threatened with every new revelation broadcast to the room.

Finally, as the day drew to a close, the presenter shared a thought that I found absurd. She claimed that TCKs tended to be *drawn* to each other. In her experience, they had an uncanny ability to find each other at social gatherings and felt more comfortable around each other – even if they had never lived in the same countries. Recognizing others who understood transience and not belonging in a normal context drew TCKs together. This sounded like a stretch to me. I certainly didn't have some sort of TCK radar. In fact, this was the first time I even had the words to express that was what I was.

Then the psychic woman asked anyone in the room who thought they were a TCK, based on her description, to raise their hands. I refused. What if she called me to the front to point out to the rest of my coworkers all the issues, psychoses, and weaknesses that 'my people' apparently had? No. Way. I sat on my hands, but I was secretly eager to see who else in the room was a TCK. Around 10 seconds passed while nobody raised their hand. I suddenly felt sorry for the presenter. Yes, she was clearly an evil mind-reader, but she had worked so hard at revealing my soul without my permission – I mean, there were even charts and graphs. In a snap of compassion, my hand shot up. I couldn't bear letting this woman think she had shared all day in vain. I waited for the rest of the room to turn and stare at me, gasp, then run for pitchforks and clubs in an attempt to capture the freak in their midst. But no angry mobs formed. Something worse happened.

From my vantage point at the back of the room, I still didn't see anyone else with a raised hand – I was the lone TCK. Then I turned to my left and recoiled in shock. The other seven people sitting at the table with me all had their hands up. The eight TCKs in the room were sitting together. I nearly blurted my anger out loud. What idiots we were, we absolutely proved her previous point. Without realizing it, we had all been drawn together just like she said. While I knew the other people at the table and considered them friends, I didn't know they were TCKs. The presenter grinned knowingly and pointed out that we had clustered together without any of us having planned to huddle in solidarity. She had won.

As one TCK recounts, *'Despite the backlash against labels and the necessity for everyone to fit into a neat box, having a delineated identity can be reassuring.'*[3] While it's certainly true some people don't want to be labeled for fear it detracts from their originality and uniqueness, labels do provide comfort and a sense of belonging. Categorizations like TCK or CCK aren't meant to box in a group of people and mark them as predictable (that really isn't possible), the terms are meant to provide context and validation. Individual identity is incredibly complex. Even if a person is a

TCK or CCK – that's not *all* they are, that's just one aspect.[6]

People are like photographs in need of the right level of zoom to be understood. Zoom too far in (or focus too much on individuality) and we fill the screen, giving no context. Zoom too far out (or focus on sweeping generalizations) and we get lost in the crowd. For a clear picture of who we really are (identity), we've got to get the zoom level (the balance between individuality and commonality) right.

If you like lists, this part's for you:

* A Cross Cultural Kid (CCK) is *'a person who is living or has lived in – or meaningfully interacted with – two or more cultural environments for a significant period of time during childhood (up to age 18)'*.[2]

* A Third Culture Kid (TCK) is *'A person who has spent a significant part of his or her developmental years outside the parents' culture. The TCK builds relationships to all of the cultures, while not having full ownership in any. Although elements from each culture are assimilated into the TCK's life experience, the sense of belonging is in relationship to others of similar experience.'*[2]

* An Invisible Alien (sometimes called a 'hidden immigrant') is someone who *'can be as culturally clueless about their supposed 'home culture' as any true immigrant, but no one will give them allowance for their ignorance, or clue them in like they would an obvious immigrant.*[4]

* *'All TCKs carry something of their host cultures within them for the rest of their lives, probably more than they realize. Our childhood experiences do shape us, and will revisit us again and again.'*[3]

* *'Perhaps the most confusing part of being a third-culture kid is the absence of a concrete identity.'*[5] Everyone struggles to figure out 'who they are' – it's an important part of the adventure of life. Having a secure sense of self gives us peace, confidence, a sense of belonging, and helps us interact with others. While CCKs and TCKs may have some additional challenges, knowing there are terms to describe our cross-cultural experience is a big help.

---

[1] *B At Home, Emma Moves Again*. Valérie Besanceney. Summertime. 2014.

[2] *Third Culture Kids, The Experience of Growing Up Among Worlds*. David C. Pollock and Ruth E. Van Reken. Nicholas Brealey America; Revised Edition. 2009.

[3] *The Worlds Within – An anthology of TCK art and writing: young, global and between cultures*. Summertime. 2014.

[4] *Belonging Everywhere & Nowhere: Insights into Counseling the Globally Mobile*. Lois J. Bushong, M.S. Mango Tree Intercultural Services. 2013.

[5] *The 3 'Third Culture Kid' Cultures* (http://libbystephens.com/blog/third-culture-kids/31-the-3-qthird-culture-kidq-cultures), Libby Stephens. 2011.

[6] *The Global Nomad's Guide To University Transition.* Tina L. Quick. Summertime. 2010.

[7] *Expat Teens Talk.* Dr. Lisa Pittman and Diana Smit. Summertime. 2012

[8] *Burn-Up or Splash Down: Surviving the Culture Shock of Re-Entry.* Marion Knell. IVP Books. 2007.

[9] *The Art of Coming Home.* Craig Storti. Intercultural Press Inc. 1997.

CHAPTER 2

THE NAKED TRUTH ABOUT RELATIONSHIPS

MAKING FRIENDS, KEEPING FRIENDS,
AND LETTING GO OF FRIENDS

A GREAT LIFE... WITH SIDE EFFECTS

One of the best discoveries I made while in the U.S. was American TV commercials – in particular drug commercials. They're unlike anything I've seen anywhere else on the planet, and they all follow a similar format – an attractive individual will complain about some sort of physical problem, illness, sickness, or condition. They will then go on to explain how this particularly heart-wrenching ailment – heartburn, for example – is wreaking havoc on their lives, preventing them from living out a full and normal existence. Then the music, lighting, and mood of the emotional mini-drama changes completely as this charming character shares with unbridled joy and excitement how, after speaking with their doctor, they've discovered a new drug that alleviates their previously debilitating heartburn.

At this point in the commercial, our newly healthy hero can be seen merrily living out their now-normal existence: meeting friends at coffee shops, leaping confidently from a diving board, reading a book at home while adoring pets cuddle closely, picking up angelic and well-behaved children from school, sky diving, preparing a three-course meal in a sleek and modern kitchen, accepting an award at a local theater group, choosing shampoo from a store – you get the idea. During this montage of happiness, a narrator soothingly explains what this marvelous medication is for and then rather deftly slips into an extensive monologue listing the horrifying potential side-effects of this wonder-drug: drowsiness, headache, diarrhea, loss of consciousness, high blood pressure, low blood pressure, anal leakage (really, I've legitimately heard that one), bleeding of the mucous membranes, loss of appetite, binge eating, paranoia, insomnia, explosion of the limbs, rapid toenail growth, discoloration of the tongue, hair loss, halitosis, fever, sores, blisters, memory loss, or possibly death. Following this terrifying monologue, the beautiful main character (who apparently dodged all of these frightful side effects) looks to the camera and encourages you to consult your doctor to see if this drug is right for you. Quite frankly, I'd rather just deal with heartburn.

It's rather an extreme example, but life is a bit like these over-the-top drug commercials: there exists the possibility for both good and bad, positive and negative effects. TCKs and CCKs have some amazing strengths they are likely to benefit from, as well as some challenges they are likely to face. Just as drug companies are obliged to inform consumers about the downsides of their wonderful medications, I feel it's easier to navigate life knowing what perks AND what pitfalls potentially lie ahead. *'Knowledge empowers us to overcome adversity.'*[1] It's important to note that while, broadly defined, CCKs have certain similarities, there exists no absolute formula that can map a personality. People vary wildly in many ways, even when they share common traits such as multicultural exposure or high mobility as they grow up. Thankfully, some marvelously clever people have managed to chart the tendencies that TCKs seem more likely to share.[2] Ultimately, if you've been brought up dosed with TCK or CCK medication, it may add some pretty amazing dynamics to your life and personality, but there may also be some potential side effects. If you know your strengths you can capitalize on them, and if you're aware of your weaknesses you can consciously address them.

ADAPTABILITY

One of the strengths that I greatly admire and routinely find among TCKs is adaptability: the capacity to change as necessary in different situations and environments. Most TCKs have had to adapt to a new school, a new country, a new set of friends, a new set of expectations, a new routine, and perhaps even a new language. I think it's fair to say that everyone in the world has to deal with change, and while the vast majority of people seem to be able to cope, some do it better than others. TCKs are subjected to far more drastic changes far more frequently than most people and this, I believe, is what supercharges their powers of adaptability. It's not always easy to take continual upheaval and change in stride (much less see them as positive experiences), but it's often these challenging events that develop useful skills and lead to unforeseen possibilities. *'The ability of the TCK to adapt to various cultures, their fluency in languages, the ability to blend in with those around them, the skills to listen and observe, and even their sense of loyalty for systems, can serve them well.'*[3]

Along with many of my fellow TCKs, I've taken advantage of the opportunity presented by a move to a new country or school to update and reinvent myself. A move can mean a fresh start. While it is certainly draining and exhausting in some ways, it does provide a chance at a clean slate socially – and that's something (believe it or not) many non-TCKs have longed for.

Let's take, for example, one of the most embarrassing events of my teenage years. I was 15 and on an amazing youth trip with 500 other high school students. I found myself under a starry sky on a beach lit by a giant moon enjoying the dancing flames of a bonfire surrounded by hundreds of teenagers from schools all over Europe. I was a freshman in high school and life really was good – how could it not be, I was on a trip with all my friends on a Mediterranean island.

Earlier, my friends and I had learned we could scoop up the dead jellyfish that washed up on the shores and fling them into the bonfire, resulting in a satisfying sizzling sound. We could justify the routine as an act of public service: nobody wanted to step on and get stung by a washed-up jellyfish. But as the evening progressed and the number of jellyfish corpses diminished, I grew ever more tired. Several days of late night beach parties followed by early mornings were wearing me down. No matter how exciting life is around you, eventually sleep creeps to the top of the list of most appealing activities.

I bid my friends good night and began the long and arduous trek to my room. All 500 or so students were housed in one large, though modest, hotel with its own beachfront access. This was the island's low season so the beach was ours. Really, the whole town and quite possibly half the island was ours – a good thing for all parties concerned. Admittedly, 500 teenagers can be slightly disruptive and overwhelming – a fun crowd to be a part of, but not a fun crowd to be invaded by.

I climbed the tall stone steps that led from the beach through the rock up to the street level above. From there it was a steep, winding uphill hike to the warmly glowing and welcoming hotel entrance. I almost stopped in the lobby for a break, but decided I needed to persevere up the four flights of uniquely tall, precarious, and narrow steps found in buildings that are beginning to show their age. The way up was slow, arduous, and good for the calf muscles and quads.

The great thing about large generic budget hotels is you can jam 500 students into them affordably without great risk of damage to anything terribly unique or irreplaceable. The bad thing about large generic budget hotels is that everything is replaceable and, well generic – looking the same. As a result, to me the third floor looked the same as the fourth floor. Being too tired to focus on door numbers and unwisely giving in to my aching legs (which assured me this was far enough to climb), I dragged myself to the end of the third floor hallway where my room would have been if I was only one floor above.

Oblivious to the digits emblazoned on the door, I opened it and wearily entered. The door was unlocked. This was good because I had no key. The hotel issued one key per room of four students and charged a ridiculously high ransom if you lost that one precious key. My roommates and I had realized the total value of all our luggage and belongings probably didn't add up to the key replacement fee, so we agreed to leave our door unlocked. Unfortunately for me, the residents of the room I had just invaded on the third floor must have had the same thought.

Ready to drop, I nearly collapsed onto the nearest bed – but I hesitated. No matter how hard you try, any time spent on a beach allows for sand to inundate the places you least expect on your body. If I got into bed without showering, I would itch all night from sand infestation. Alone in the room, I sighed and dragged myself to the bathroom. Focusing intently on getting to bed, I clawed my clothes off and fell into the shower. As I rinsed away the alarming amount sand I was discovering on my person, I realized I couldn't find my shampoo or soap. Too tired to analyze this further, I finished de-sanding and got out of the shower only to discover I couldn't find my towel either.

For the first time that evening, alarm bells went off in my head. Sadly, they weren't the right set of alarm bells. My roommates and I had learned early on in the week that the generous balconies our corner room afforded us were perfect for an immature, yet sadly satisfying prank. We would conceal each other's luggage, toiletries, clothing, etc. out on the balcony, hidden at the far corner where it could not be seen from inside the large sliding glass windows – even if you pulled the curtains back. We'd taken the prank so far as to move one roommate's entire bed to the hidden corner and convince him he'd been reassigned to a broom closet on the eighth floor.

Now, as I stood naked and dripping in the bathroom unable to locate my towel, I assumed my mischievous roommates had simply hidden my currently much-needed items on the balcony. What a waste, I thought, they weren't even in the room to enjoy the fruits of their labor. I grudgingly plodded out onto the balcony, dripping all the way across the floor. The outside air chilled me, but not as much as the stark realization that not a single item was out on the balcony with me. Not my towel or toiletries, nor anything else.

I stood there, cold and trying to wrap my exhausted mind around my predicament when I heard the door to the room open. I felt relieved – now I could get my friends to turn over my belongings after they had a good laugh at the fact I was out on the balcony naked. But when I rounded the corner and reached for the sliding glass door handle, I did not catch a glimpse of my roommates. In fact, I didn't recognize the three people who had just entered the room at all. Shocked, I leapt back into the obscure corner.

We were being robbed! It suddenly seemed obvious to me – these guys knew most people were out on the beach until late so they'd snuck into our room to steal our belongings. I panicked. I glanced around for inspiration, strength – something. Finally, a flash of bravery hit me: I should leap into the room and stun them. It would definitely catch them off guard. They'd run screaming, and I'd be a hero – a naked hero. I wasn't really sure if that was an upgrade from regular hero, but I was willing to risk it.

Having decided on this overly valiant but underly clothed course of action, I stood ready to heave open the sliding glass door and stun the intruders inside. In that raw and tense moment of preparation, doubt began to take hold: what if they were violent thieves? What if the shock of the situation didn't so much alarm them as enrage them? I imagine, even if it's only psychological, one feels better positioned to ward off attacks when one is fully clothed. Desperate for something to make sense, I surveyed the ground below – the familiar plants of the hotel's modest garden were shrouded in the faint light of the moon, dark, familiar, and... bigger than I remembered. "Wow, those plants have grown quickly!" I thought.

For the second time that evening, alarm bells rang in my head. I realized the plants had not benefited from a sudden growth spurt, they merely appeared bigger because I was closer to them. Closer, because this was not the fourth floor and, therefore, not my balcony. It finally hit me. I was not being invaded by mysterious intruders. I was the intruder – a naked, confused, and trapped intruder.

Panic and fear washed over me more forcibly than when I thought I was being robbed. What was I to do? After frantically searching for any means available to climb the three meters that separated the balcony I was on from the balcony I so desperately wanted to be on, I concluded there was no way. I would still be forced to go into the room. Could I just wait until the three guys fell asleep? Visions ran through my head of what any one of them would think of waking up suddenly in the night to a naked man entering their room from the balcony... There was no way it would end well; viewers just tuning in would certainly misconstrue the situation.

I knew what I needed to do, but what on earth was I going to say when I got in there? I would have to calmly and nakedly explain things. If I addressed the situation unflustered, perhaps they would remain unfazed as well. The trouble was, I had pondered and hesitated for far too long. Finally, in a moment of brief and overzealous gusto, I threw open the sliding glass door. It rivaled the climactic moment of any TV soap opera where someone enters a room with overstated purpose as the music swells and everyone gasps in amazement...

Unfortunately for me, the swelling music was only in my head – though my sudden and inexplicably forceful entrance to the room did draw gasps from the three residents I barged in on. From there, things did not go at all as planned. The three guys who found themselves confronted with my abrupt and naked entrance did not run off screaming or leap on me violently. After the initial gasp, they simply sat where they were, staring – not moving, barely breathing – just staring. I too was barely breathing and simply staring, but they had more to look at than I did. Words failed me. I simply stood in vulnerable silence.

After what seemed like hours (but in reality couldn't have been more than a minute) in this ludicrously frozen impasse, I decided it was time to exit this clearly humiliating situation. Unable to focus on anything but my single-minded resolution to get out, I walked calmly and without emotion to the door and disappeared from the room into the hallway. Out of sight from the stunned faces, I began to realize my situation had not really improved much. I was now naked in the hallway. I was willing to scamper down the hall, up the stairs, and down the corresponding hallway one floor above to reach my own room. But there was a problem with this plan: my wallet was in the front pocket of the shorts that currently lay crumpled in these poor boys' bathroom.

I needed my wallet – not only did it have all my money, it contained a way to positively ID me as the strange invader. The wallet would have to be retrieved.

Without thinking much more into things (I didn't want to build up another bout of over-the-top-entrance-gusto) I nonchalantly reentered the room to find three stunned faces in the exact position I'd left them moments ago. I proceeded, unfazed, into the bathroom, put on my clothes, and walked calmly back out the door – noting on my way out that the room's inhabitants had not so much as shifted position or closed their gaping mouths.

Clothed and feeling somewhat triumphant, I climbed the steep stairs to the appropriate floor and finally made it to my own room. By this time, the rest of my roommates were already in bed and a little curious as to where I'd been. I wasn't entirely sure how to explain, so I didn't. As I drifted off to sleep I felt a certain sense of pride – the night could have ended a lot worse. I was relatively unscathed and nobody was any the wiser.

That sense of triumphant pride did not last long. By the next day, word of a strange (if not possibly dangerous) boy and his late night nude breaking-and-entering escapades spread throughout the camp. Admittedly, the unintended victims of my intrusion couldn't possibly be expected to keep such a bizarre evening to themselves. Their version lacked some basic facts, but then they never did get exposed to the full story, just to the full... me.

Even after rather publicly pointing me out on the beach, the guys from the room below could never be completely sure I was the intruder. Their accusations were enough, however, to instigate rumors and legends about me that necessitated a lot of difficult explanations to my friends and adult leaders. How on earth was I going to convince all the people I knew that it was a perfectly innocent mistake and avoid being labeled as 'stripper boy' for the rest of my high school career?

Hitting the Reset Button

There ended up being a very simple fix: I moved. Shortly after the trip ended, my family relocated and I was afforded a clean slate. Of course that clean slate came at the cost of losing all my friends and once again having to make new ones, but in some ways the reset was useful. A clean slate can be an opportunity to reinvent oneself. I honestly believe it's one of the reasons some people who grow up in transience tend to be amazingly socially capable and good with people. They get the opportunity to learn from each move and to use what they've learned to create a newer version of themselves. If something about you worked well in one place, you could emphasize those attributes in your next home. Similarly, if something about you didn't attract the sort of attention or get the desired results, you could reinvent yourself without those traits in your next home – and none of your new friends would ever be the wiser. In essence, people who move around a lot while growing up (or who have people around them move a lot) get the unique opportunity to constantly refine their personality and social skills. While most people are unavoidably connected with their past and how people remember them, many TCKs get to advance through life with multiple social memory resets.

While this certainly does mean TCKs are often more able to refine how other people see and interact with them, it also means the valuable currency of social history is often wiped out. Usually, a move means *'you have lost your status, roles, and routines, and the comfort and self-confidence that go along with them.'*[1] Starting from scratch allows reinvention, but it also means the social stock market crashes frequently, virtually erasing all the value and investment that's been put in. For some TCKs, the frequent social stock market crashes are devastating enough that they don't bother reinventing themselves. It's easier to simply brace for the inevitable collapse; why build up and invest in something that's just going to be wiped out?

So, while there may be some perks to getting to be the new kid and having a fresh start, most would agree it's also pretty draining at times. In reality, it's not healthy to just run (or move) away from problems. Issues and struggles can often follow us through a move. Being adaptable means understanding that *'new experiences becoming a part of you do not mean your old ones get erased'*.[4] We may not be able to change the fact that we're moving, but we can at least make sure we leave well and address challenges rather than flee from them. In the book, *Third Culture Kids: The Experience of Growing Up Between Worlds*, co-authors Ruth E. Van Reken and Dave Pollock had a quick and useful acronym for a good checklist on how to leave well: R.A.F.T.[2]

R: Reconciliation. Don't leave with unfinished business or unresolved issues. Ask forgiveness, clear up misunderstandings, and apologize if necessary.

A: Affirmation. Let people know you appreciate them. It may sound overly sentimental, but you'll feel better knowing you told loved ones they are just that: loved.

F: Farewells. Say goodbye to people. In fact, say goodbye to places, pets, and even possessions. There's something inside us that is able to move on more easily when we know goodbyes have been said.

T: Think Destination. Now that you've brought closure to a chapter of life that will forever be part of your story, you can start focusing on the adventures to come.

Even if done well, moving (or having everyone else around you move) and continual transition can make it difficult to have a clear sense of self amidst such constant reinvention. Of course, everyone is refining who they are and developing their personality as they grow older. But the ability to do so with regular 'resets' freeing you from the anchor of old versions of self can leave a person feeling they're so adaptable and so chameleon-like that they don't know who they really are underneath it all. *'Being able to 'turn on a dime' to meet whatever situation or culture facing you is a useful skill, but doing so without a grounding in who you are can, I think, leave you feeling hollow.'*[5] I have come to believe that an understanding of core identity is incredibly important, and being able to keep a handle on who you are while adapting actually helps people to adapt better. (More on this later.) Perhaps even more so than non-TCKs, TCKs have to devote some intentional thought to who we really are. What do we really stand for? Being able to name these things is a tremendous help in being anchored in our core identity.

Guardedness

Another commonly found attribute in TCKs is a strong degree of guardedness. The move that saved me from carrying around the unfortunate nickname of 'stripper boy' occurred because the military installation I had been living on closed. The whole world I had known and lived in for the previous three years deteriorated before my eyes. Housing areas once vibrant with friends turned into abandoned ghost towns. Chris, one of the few friends I had left as the population dwindled, lived on the other side of the base from me. Journeying to see him on my bike felt like crossing the set of some sort of disaster movie. Abandoned houses, shops, and offices along the way were a stark reminder of the life seeping out of the community. The AAFES (Army Air Force Exchange Service) stores that served the few remaining personnel and their families did so with severely restricted hours and products. As the school year drew to a close, fewer and fewer students remained. Those of us still there on the very last day of school for Woodbridge American High School gathered in the auditorium to bid farewell to each other, the school and its legacy. I had performed in school plays on the stage in that very auditorium packed with hundreds of students, parents, and teachers. On the last day, there were so few of us remaining that the building seemed quite empty and excessively spacious for such a small group. Once we left, the school would sit empty and forlorn, never to be used again. Roads became overgrown with weeds. The runway that once launched noisy A-10 fighter aircraft over my head was no longer a restricted area – my sisters and I could run our dog,

Tillie, up and down the abandoned tarmac with no fear of armed guards or anybody paying the slightest bit of attention to us.

When we finally left the closing base (we were among the last group of families to leave the housing area) I remember feeling not only sad, but insignificant. So many memories had been built, so much time invested in that place – and it withered and died on me. Friends I previously couldn't imagine living without were flung thousands of kilometers away. Yes, we'd try to keep in touch, but we all knew it wouldn't be the same. I felt like the shriveling base. Despite all the life and energy that once surrounded me, I was left with little to show for it. Of course those friendships, memories, and interactions helped shape who I am today, but at the time I didn't feel that way, and I moved to our next home with resolute guardedness. I didn't like the feeling of having everything and everyone taken away, and as it was inevitably going to happen again, I was going to guard against it. If every 'hello' is just a 'goodbye' waiting to happen, why even waste time with 'hello'?

Thankfully, I was able to grow past my initial guardedness. Certainly not immediately, but over time. Energized by the new world I was a part of, I began to appreciate the importance of 'now'. (More on this later as well.) Yes, every 'hello' did ultimately lead to a 'goodbye', but in between the two was crammed the magic of relationships. We are built for relationship; it's a fundamental part of being human.

The deep end

It's fair to say that not only did I get over my guardedness against relationships – I excelled in them. I found myself engaging with others through another tendency TCKs often develop: diving in deep. Most relationships seem to follow a natural progression. People meet, begin spending time together – usually in groups – then progress to the point where they're comfortable together without a group. This, over time, leads to self-disclosure and sharing. Whether it's a friendship, a dating relationship, or even a marriage, you can't help but admire the people who know each other so well as to finish each other's thoughts or predict each other's needs. We all want that. We want to know and be known; it's human nature.

My view on relationships as temporary and fleeting (shaped to a strong degree by various moves) had initially made me guarded against allowing anyone to get too close, so I could avoid the pain of goodbyes. But the emptiness left in place of friendships needed to be filled. Not long after my move from R.A.F. Woodbridge, the closed military base in the U.K., I decided, very intentionally, to fill the emptiness with as many deep relationships as possible.

I couldn't waste time with all the pleasantries of getting to know someone and waiting for the lead-up to depth and self-disclosure. If I was going to only have someone as a friend for a short while, I wanted that entire short while to be spent at the deep level. Rather than dip my toes in and progressively lower myself into the waters of mutual association, I was hurling myself off the high dive board without even having prepped enough to take my clothes off and put on proper swimming attire. I launched into friendships with what must have been alarming voracity. I could transition from complete stranger to closest and bestest friend in the course of a week.

Looking back and having discussed this trend with many fellow TCKs, I've realized that the 'diving in deep' approach is the opposite side of the same defense mechanism: guardedness. It's an attempt to cope with transient friendships and the instability they highlight. In some ways, diving in deep is easy because relationships are fleeting. If you bear all of your heart and soul to someone and they reject it, they're not sticking around too long anyway (or you're not); the possibility of rejection doesn't sting as much. Ironically, both guarding ourselves from people and throwing ourselves into the deep end too quickly run the risk of viewing other people more as commodities than as actual people.

Guardedness demeans people. Taken to the extreme, it's like reducing them to assailants that will hurt us – shifty characters lurking in plain sight waiting to gain our trust and then abandon us – laughing maniacally as they fling discarded mementos of our time together from the plane that carries them away from us... even though hurling objects from a plane is both difficult (passenger windows don't open on commercial jets these days) and almost certainly illegal and dangerous.

On the other end of the spectrum, jumping into instant depth with people is like attacking them and trying to suck out all the richness as quickly as possible for our own nourishment. We become friendship vampires. Having dined heartily on the emotional bonding of an innocent bystander and then abandoning them as an exhausted carcass, we retreat to our caves and grow stronger from the deep revelations coursing through us. Content for now, we will sleep. But when we awake we will once again be wracked by the insatiable desire for depth. Perhaps some fresh new student will arrive tomorrow. We must pounce on them before anyone else does.

Okay, those may be slightly overstated examples, but you get my point. I've learned the healthiest thing anyone can do with regard to friendships is to remember that ultimately everyone is looking for the same thing: to love and be loved for who we are, not as a commodity or a disposable toy. Some of the best approaches for finding the right balance with relationships and avoiding either the 'guard against assailants' or 'friendship vampire' extremes are ones we learned (hopefully) as small children. Be genuine, don't be fake; be a good listener; be reliable; think about the needs of others before your own; be humble.[1] They sound cliché and obvious, but those classic instructions, when consciously heeded with a measure of patience, truly can help form healthy friendships. Friends will come and go, and we've got to enjoy them while we've got them. Believe it or not, some will stand the test of time. We must enjoy the depth that's *earned*. Heartache and loss will come, but in the wise words of Kahlil Gilbran, *'The deeper that sorrow carves into your being, the more joy you can contain. Is not the cup that holds your wine the very cup that was burned in the potter's oven?'*[6]

TOO POPULAR?

In some respects, it can seem as if TCKs have an overabundance of friendships. Most TCKs I know have vastly more friends on Facebook than their non-transient counterparts. I'd love to say it's because TCKs are endowed with irresistible magnetic charm and so they naturally have a vast teeming plethora of friends. Perhaps there's some truth to that (clearly, we're amazing), but the reality is far more mathematically simple. Most TCKs move a lot and those around them move a lot – we're simply exposed to a lot of people.

This extensive relationship bank is a truly envious asset. I am fortunate enough to have such a widely spread group of friends that I can travel to many parts of the world and have a friend to stay with in the area. I save a lot of money on hotels. I am also not blind to the fact that many opportunities in life come about because of the people we know. Many striving businessmen would kill for the expansive list of social contacts TCKs can establish as they grow up. It truly is an advantage to have – not only as a means of free accommodation while traveling, but also for strategic contacts and global networking.

Ironically, this highly sought-after advantage can also feel like a disadvantage. One student I know remarked to me that he hated Facebook. It made his life complicated. I couldn't understand; for TCKs, social networking tools like Facebook are a lifeline to stay in touch with friends we've made who now live all over the world. All the research points to the fact that social networking is ideal for TCKs, almost built precisely for us. I assured him he was wrong, he needed to love Facebook and not find it a burden – the research said so.

He continued to protest and explained that the amount of friends he was connected to was overwhelming. With each move he was faced with the difficult task of deciding how to spend his time. With so many friends on Facebook from the many places he'd lived and all the people who had moved in and out of his life, trying to keep in touch with all of them was impossible. He wanted to make new friends but felt this often took time away from keeping in touch with old friends. There's only so much time in a day, who do you spend it with? Investing in new friends at the expense of old ones? With those you've known the longest? With those you just moved away from or who just moved away from you?

In reality, we as humans only have so much capacity for relationship. If we go overboard on quantity we sacrifice quality. It's a hard balance to maintain and I have to admit I haven't found an easy way to prioritize friendships. There is no easy answer. As a TCK, the question of how we prioritize the often-overwhelming amount of relationships we're fortunate enough to collect is one that needs to be tackled with our own experience, preference, and personality. Over and over again experts and other TCKs seem to agree that keeping in touch with previous friends is essential.[4] Whether during transition or even in-between transitions, maintaining long-term friendships should be a priority.

KEEP IT REAL

At the same time, *'today's world of social media has helped enormously, but a new challenge facing some is to make 'in-person' friends in a new place rather than spend all of their time on Facebook with friends from a previous location.'*[3] Social media has come so far and done so much to help people keep in touch. It's also brought with it new difficulties. For one thing, we have an online presence to look after. Back in the days of old (before Facebook), people didn't have to worry about the balance between personal disclosure and public relations – that was a problem reserved mostly for famous people. But now, managing our public image is a fact of life. We suddenly have access to millions of potential viewers, readers, followers and stalkers. We're not so much *acting* like we're 'on stage' now, in some ways, we *are* on a giant stage constantly being recorded – and that can be a little overwhelming.

My dear friend, Karen, was once a kindergarten teacher. Karen truly has a larger-than-life personality so she must have been an amazingly fun teacher. During her time as an educator of small children she took it upon herself to train her students that whenever she entered the room, they should stand and applaud her arrival. It was really a joke for Karen's entertainment, but the kids quite happily went along with it. So day in and day out, Karen would enter her kindergarten classroom to an uproarious standing ovation from a gaggle of giggling students. In response to this fanfare, Karen would saunter to her desk, waving and blowing kisses to her adoring fans. This was everyday life for Karen and her class.

At some point in the school year, the entire student body was gathered together in the gym for a presentation. Being the smallest of children present, the kindergarten classes were right in the front, seated in neat rows at the feet of whoever was addressing the school. Karen stood dutifully on the side of the gym watching over her children and ensuring they paid proper respect to the adults in front of them. In the midst of the presentation, Karen received an important phone call and quietly stepped out of the gym to take the call. Having dealt with whatever needed her attention, she crept back into the gym, trying to enter unnoticed and not distract from the assembly in progress.

But Karen had trained her students too well. All it took was for one or two of her perceptive students to see her enter the gym and they responded in a Pavlovian fashion by leaping to their feet and applauding loudly. At once, several things happened. The rest of Karen's class jumped to their feet and joined in the applause. This in turn caused the other kindergarten classes to do the same, followed by a wave of older students, row after row behind them, until the entire student body was applauding loudly (without even quite knowing why). The speaker was terribly confused as he wasn't aware that he'd finished. Karen took the whole fiasco in stride and marched across the front of the gym waving gratefully in response to the school-wide applause. Reaching the other side of the gym, she motioned for the students to sit (and they did), then motioned for the presenter to go on presenting (and he did).

We're far more like Karen's students than we realize. Social media has trained us to seek followers and to follow. If we're not careful, we can stop investing in real relationships and devote all our social time and energy to cultivating fans. Fans aren't really able to give us what we need out of a healthy relationship. Neither do they inspire us to be what others need. Don't get me wrong, I get just as excited as the next guy when I have a new 'like', but it's worth bearing in mind that our new-found ability to be famous in our own world is an *addition to* and not a *replacement for* meaningful relationships.

Keeping old friends and making new ones requires balance. It's also important to understand it's natural to have limits; no one can maintain good quality deep relationships with a vast number of people. We're not built that way. The key is knowing your limits and operating within them. Otherwise, we run the risk of sacrificing old friends for new ones and never building up a valuable history with people. Or we live in the past and never develop much needed real-life relationships in the present. We've got to find the balance that works for us. Life takes place amidst a network of relationships, and we discover a lot about who we are when we examine who our friends are.

IF YOU LIKE LISTS, THIS PART'S FOR YOU:

* Being a TCK or CCK (like being part of *any* culture) comes with both strengths and challenges.

* TCKs tend to be very adaptable. *'The ability of the TCK to adapt to various cultures, their fluency in languages, the ability to blend in with those around them, the skills to listen and observe, and even their sense of loyalty for systems, can serve them well.'*[3]

* Frequent moves may give the ability to clear your slate or reinvent yourself. But the constant change can also make it hard to determine who you really are amidst all the adaptation.

* A helpful checklist for leaving well (which also helps you enter a new place well) is R.A.F.T.: Reconcile (don't leave unfinished business with people), Affirm (let people know what they meant to you), Farewell (say goodbye to significant people, places, and things), Think Destination (move forward).[2]

* As a result of frequent goodbyes, TCKs can be guarded against forming relationships or dive in deep and quickly to relationships.

* Remember, people want what you do: to be loved and known, and not seen as a toy or commodity. As silly as it sounds, consciously applying all the basics you learned as a small child to make friends (be genuine, be humble, think of others needs first, be a good listener, etc.) can help you form real, lasting, and meaningful friendships.

* Because of frequent moves, TCKs are exposed to a lot of people. It can be frustrating to try and keep up with everyone and make new friends as well. Remember experts and fellow TCKs alike agree that keeping in touch with past friends is very important.[4] At the same time, a balance must be struck so you're able to engage with friends in real life where you are and not live exclusively online with friends from the past.[3]

[1] *The Global Nomad's Guide To University Transition.* Tina L. Quick. Summertime. 2010.

[2] *Third Culture Kids, The Experience of Growing Up Among Worlds.* David C. Pollock and Ruth E. Van Reken. Nicholas Brealey America; Revised Edition. 2009.

[3] *Belonging Everywhere & Nowhere: Insights into Counseling the Globally Mobile.* Lois J. Bushong, M.S. M.S. Mango Tree Intercultural Services. 2013.

[4] *Expat Teens Talk.* Dr. Lisa Pittman and Diana Smit. Summertime. 2012.

[5] *The Worlds Within – An anthology of TCK art and writing: young, global and between cultures.* Summertime. 2014.

[6] *The Prophet.* Kahlil Gibran. 1923.

The Naked Truth about Relationships

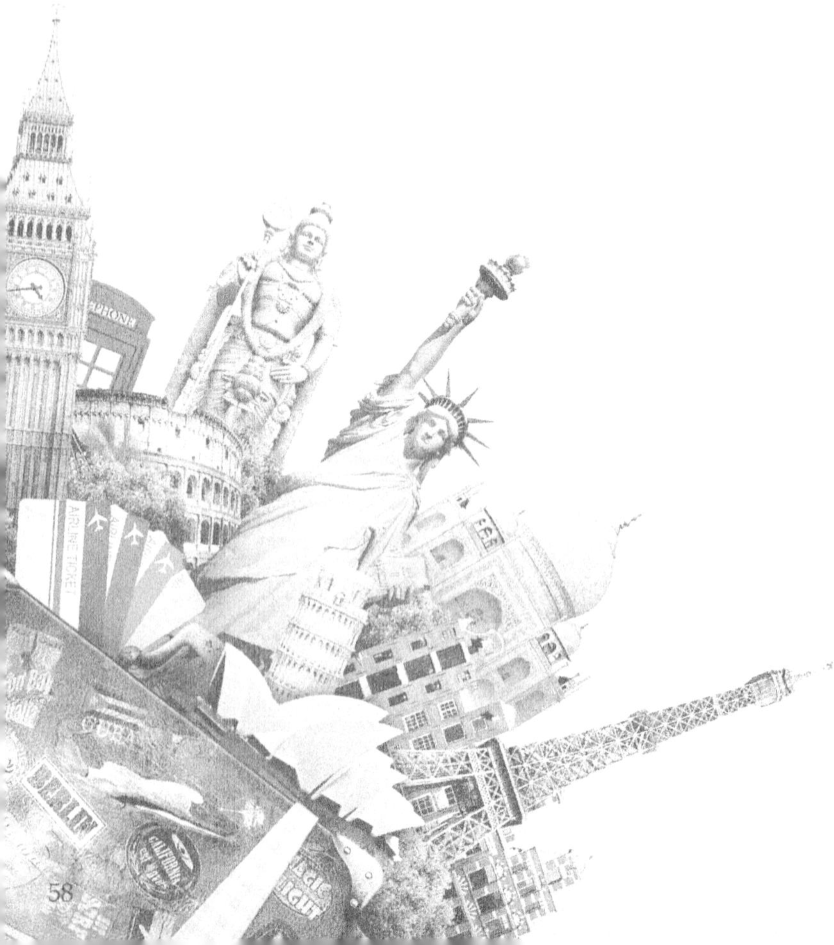
AIRLINE TICKET
BERLIN

CHAPTER 3

DON'T RUN...
USE YOUR WORDS

CONFLICT RESOLUTION
AND COMMUNICATION

Arrivals and Departures

When I was 29 I went on an adventure to the Balkans with my intrepid friend, Luke. I've known Luke for a long time, and he's a great travel companion, partially because he's strong as an ox and can look very intimidating; but also because he's willing to travel off the beaten path. One of our last stops on this particular journey was the beautiful beach-laden city of Budva in Montenegro. Our time in Budva presented a challenge that neither Luke's strength nor my charming accent could combat. The city was on fire. Amazingly, the locals were not overly panicked. I, however, felt some degree of concern that the flames were getting bigger and the smoke thicker. Not to mention the general path of said raging inferno was eating through buildings along the sloping mountains surrounding us, heading toward our current coastal refuge. Other than knowing the fires began in the forests surrounding the city, nobody could tell us the origin of the blaze coming towards us.

Luke and I were already planning on leaving Montenegro and heading to Sarajevo in Bosnia Herzegovina, and this seemed all the more a good decision since (to the best of our knowledge), Sarajevo was not on fire. To expedite our evacuation, we made our way to the Budva Bus Station. Apparently, in a custom that differs considerably from those in Western Europe, bus stations in Montenegro also double as nightclubs. We arrived to throngs of people packed tightly in a confined platform trying their best to shake their respective groove things despite the space constraints. Loud thumping techno music surrounded us and completely drowned out the feeble attempts at announcements made to herald incoming or outgoing buses in a language apparently comprehensible to no one.

Buses pulled into the station and passengers disembarked, melding into the oscillating crowd. Simultaneously, sweat-soaked dancers entered buses and were transported to... other night club/bus stations, presumably. Not speaking any of the Balkan dialects, Luke and I tried to locate some sort of explanatory departures board, information sign, schedule, or even cryptic runes scrawled in living rock. There were none. We spent the next hour frantically dashing from bus to bus (unintentionally starting conga-lines in some cases) trying to find a vehicle indicating our destination.

Finally, well over an hour after its alleged departure time, an archaic vehicle bearing a resemblance to what might be a precursor to modern-day buses heaved painfully into view. Luke and I shuddered at the possibility we might have to board this horrifying infraction of structural integrity. Surely it had been brought here to die, or to serve as a mobile toilet facility (it looked like it had gained some experience as such already).

Sadly, scrawled across what must have at one time been a relatively transparent but now grimily opaque windshield was the word 'Sarajevo.' This mobile latrine would evidently be responsible for conveying us from fun but-flaming Budva to pleasantly not-on-fire Sarajevo.

Probably due in part to the bus being so late, possibly because the city was on fire, and possibly because of the energy in the crowd around us, people were clearly intent on boarding the bus quickly. They stormed it with all the fervor, ferocity, and self-preservation-driven fortitude of a pack of crazed bears who have been starved for an extended period of time, taunted by the smell of meat, and decorated with large bulky pieces of luggage tethered to their extremities. Luke and I nearly lost our lives in the stampede.

We finally made it onto the bus where we discovered the true meaning of biohazard contamination area. Luke and I took a seat toward the back of the bus just behind the lowered rear exit doors. The windows were remnant of petri dishes ripe with toxic cultures; the seats were cushioned with several layers of grime, expunged skin cells, excreted waste, and viral fodder. Every gap and crevice was packed and teeming with mold and countless microcosms of bacterial life.

We sat rigid in our seats. We were terrified at the thought of falling asleep and slouching against a window or other surface, only to be wrenched awake with the writhing anguish of our flesh melting away and providing the necessary nutrients to expand the universe of bacteria we had become guests in. As the bus started, we became painfully aware we had chosen seats in the direct path of the singular heating vent on the vehicle. By the end of the journey my legs had been cooked evenly into brisket – they would have gone well with steak sauce, but would be utterly useless as a means of conveyance. Not long after our departure, we also learned that in an act of engineering cruelty (with no regard for health or safety) the heating vent was quite possibly just an exhaust vent pointing inside the bus. We spent the next 10 hours breathing diesel fumes and wondering whether the conversations we were having with the spores on the window were real or the result of diesel-fueled hallucinations.

The journey proceeded at a snail's pace with one headlight. Our bus driver seemed convinced that chain-smoking and allowing his second-hand smoke to fill the bus could only complement the fragrant diesel air. I must admit the bacteria, mold, and spores we rode with had to be very resilient to survive such a hostile environment. If they didn't kill me, they would probably really enhance my immune system.

The hours blended on in our asphyxiating stupor until light appeared and revealed the richly historical buildings that signified entry into the charming city of Sarajevo. At that point, we could have arrived to a firing squad perched on an island surrounded by rising molten lava while loudspeakers serenaded us with the screeches of cats in anguish – we would have still leapt off our bus with glee!

Fight or flight

Believe it or not, chances are that as TCKs, we've all been there. I don't mean we've all been to Budva while it's on fire and escaped on a precarious bus, but we've more than likely fled a situation we've deemed difficult to stay in, even if fleeing causes some degree of damage to us (or possibly those around us). In the case of Budva, I really didn't see any benefit to staying. It's a lovely place – quite beautiful – but once it caught on fire, I wasn't invested enough or equipped at all to stay and try to preserve it. I had to flee. I've found that as TCKs, we can have a tendency to do the same thing with relationships.

Because many of us grow up with some degree of transience – places, cultures, and people regularly changing around us – we tend to become (as mentioned previously) relationally guarded. We try to make letting go of people easier so we don't have to drag around an awful lot of grief[1]. Unfortunately, very few people know how to deal with grief well (TCK or otherwise). We tend to build defenses that aren't always the healthiest ways to ward off sadness.

One such mechanism is making relationships disposable. When people come into our lives, we may operate as if everyone has a sell-by date. We can enter into a relationship with the end in sight. In fact, I'd go so far as to say that sometimes we'd rather orchestrate that end (and therefore have some control over the loss we're destined to feel) rather than be at the mercy of fate. In my experience, this gives TCKs a pretty bad grasp on conflict resolution skills. *'Some TCKs never learn to deal with conflict because they know if they simply outwait the situation, or ignore it, they or the other person or persons will be gone. Then no one has to 'worry about it' anymore. This does not serve well in adulthood where conflict management in careers as well as home is a needed skill.'*[2]

For some TCKs, the idea that even if there's conflict in a relationship it can be salvaged is a strange and foreign one. In the ever-changing often-disposable world of the TCK, why fix something that's broken if you can just replace it? As I've mentioned before, this is another result of reducing people to commodities. The more I interacted with non-TCKs, the more I realized that seeing people as disposable (especially when it comes to conflict) should not be the norm.

In some ways, reaching the point in a relationship where conflict occurs is a good thing – it means you're willing to reveal more than just the polished, likable version of yourself. That may not actually be a good time to call it quits. It would mean you miss out on what it's like to work through differences and be liked – loved even – for who you are, rather than who you can appear to be. There's great depth to be grasped if we're willing to invest in someone even when we don't see eye-to-eye on everything. But that does require viewing relationships as works-in-progress, capable of being mended, rather than short-term endeavors to be abandoned when things get rough. *'Conflicts are a normal and natural part of everyone's life. Conflicts are simply the disputes and disagreements that occur between two people. While we tend to think of conflict only in terms of its negative effects, the fact is that conflict can also be positive. Without conflict there is no growth or progress.'*[3]

In a practical sense being a mediator for others in conflict is a surprisingly effective way to realize skills you can use as well. It's often easier to sort other people out rather than sort ourselves out, so learn from helping others. In her book, Tina Quick points out three elements to be aware of in situations of conflict[4]:

The **story** of what happened that triggered the conflict. Never underestimate the importance of knowing the context around a situation. No action, incident, or behavior is without a history.

The **feelings** that are generated by the conflict. Sometimes we refuse to admit the feelings fueling our side of a conflict or fail to take into account the feelings fueling someone else's side. Our words don't always convey (and sometimes even try to hide) the feelings at the heart of a matter.

The **identities** of the people involved. We all see ourselves in a certain way and can get very protective if our self-perception is threatened. If you see yourself as a generous person and someone portrays you another way in an argument, it's going to cause friction. Sometimes the root cause of a conflict has more to do with a perceived attack on a person's identity than anything else.

I FEEL YOUR PAIN

In order to resolve conflict, and not just run away from it or avoid it, we need empathy. Empathy is simply the ability to understand and share the feelings of others. Empathy allows us to connect with other people in deep and meaningful ways. It means we are not emotionally alone. It's a very powerful ability and sadly, one that seems to be on the decline. A recent study found that college students today are 40% less empathetic than they were in 1979, with the steepest decline coming in the last 10 years.[5]

Perhaps there's less empathy in the world as a defense mechanism. Perhaps it's a response to being overwhelmed by the amount of global pain and suffering we're now aware of thanks to modern technology and mass media. We definitely do have access to more information, more news, and more of what the world is experiencing than we ever have before. It is an overwhelming prospect to know so much. There is a lot of pain and suffering in the world; perhaps so much that we learn to numb ourselves in order to keep from being overwhelmed. One of the dangerous side effects in doing so is to become numb not only to remote events and situations, but also to those close by and in our immediate lives. We can't resolve conflict in relationships if we're numb. A useful way to fight being numb is to be vulnerable. As terrifying as it sounds, honestly sharing your own feelings builds a conduit with others and encourages them to do the same. It's pretty hard to be vulnerable and numb at the same time.

The Internet effect

I also believe that the amount of faceless (not direct person-to-person) communication we engage in has had an effect on our empathy. We have so many ways to be in touch with people now, but in some ways this is actually keeping us out of 'touch.' When you talk to someone face-to-face, you can react to them immediately. You can adjust your tone based on theirs, you can see when you're understood and when you're not. We tend to be more careful in actual personal interaction because we deal with the consequences immediately.

Online communication is different. On one hand, we can be more calculated – we're not under pressure to act immediately, so we can take time to formulate what we want to say. We can painstakingly perfect what we want to update as our status so that it's just witty enough to catch peoples' attention. On the other hand, we can be far more flippant. It's so easy to blurt something out, and once it's out there on the Internet, it's very hard to take back. What we post online is not that easy to delete; it's recorded, potentially forever.

Without the instant ability to see people's reactions (in their facial expressions, tone, mannerisms, etc.) and adapt accordingly, our typed words can be interpreted differently than we intend. Perhaps people read more into our words, take them more severely than we meant them, or don't understand that we're joking. If we read something and it hurts us, it could be a while before we have an opportunity to resolve it. That's time we get to spend stewing over the hurt and building up defenses, possibly even resentment, until we are able to confront the author of that hurt... if we ever do.

This is part of the reason I believe online communication is dampening our ability to have empathy. As 'instant' as we think messaging, posting, tweeting, etc. is, it's only instant in our ability to put it out. It's far less instant in its ability to be received. You can read a message when you want to – it's waiting for you at your convenience. But that very convenience opens the doors to misinterpretation.

As TCKs and CCKs, we have more opportunities (and more need) by moving through different cultures and meeting different people to take in the feelings of those around us[1]. We've got more chances to hone our empathy skills, and I think we need to take advantage of that. We've got to be willing to look at situations from someone else's perspective, and be patient enough to work through a disagreement, fight, or argument. It doesn't mean always giving in, or always winning. It means being willing to collaborate and even compromise when necessary. Sometimes it's better to stay and help fight fires to preserve a good thing than to escape by any means possible (like a hazardously filthy bus-ride). It's true some relationships must come to an end, and some points of contention are deal-breakers – but flight shouldn't always be our default response.

IT'S GOOD TO TALK

Relationships require communication, and communication is complex. As TCKs we're often pretty good at taking in information – for the most part. Generally, our adaptability can make us more aware of cultural differences and nuances. It's a matter of necessity often honed by trial and error (sometimes through great embarrassment or pain). Exposure to different cultures teaches us that there are many ways to accomplish something and rarely is there just one 'right' way. For example, universally people need to eat. But the varying ways of doing so involve different utensils and etiquette; there are countless ways to approach this common necessity. Cutlery, hands, or chopsticks; eating all the food on your plate to indicate you want more or to indicate you're finished; hands resting on the table or in the lap... there are a lot of dining options. Realizing that 'my way is not always the only/right way' is important and absolutely critical in an ever-globalizing world.

TCKs, like everyone else, make mistakes, commit *faux pas*, and must learn from mistakes. In reality, TCKs often simply have a wider playing field on which to muddle through the trials and errors of communication than other people. For my part, I have an embarrassing excess of examples that have shaped whatever cultural awareness and ability to communicate I've managed to muster.

Lost in Translation

One particular trial (and error) in Eastern Europe led to a memorable lesson in varying communication styles. I was 25 and had been assigned the role of site leader during a humanitarian service project involving high school students from across Europe. We were gathered in Slovakia and assigned to various construction tasks in various villages and towns. I should point out I have absolutely no expertise when it comes to construction. I am exceptionally lacking in any sort of skill involving coordination, dexterity, or physical prowess. While most people have the ability to command their limbs and appendages to move at will, controlled by a clever system of neural pathways and muscle memory, I seem to have what can only be described as frequent neural traffic jams and muscle amnesia. My brain may dutifully convey a command for my legs to move, but somewhere between brain and leg the signal is delayed, reinterpreted, or sometimes forgotten.

As such, my job as site leader meant that I was not in charge of completing construction (thank goodness). Rather, I was overseeing the execution of an entire work site devoted to building a new playground for a school in the Slovakian countryside. This I could handle. I had several construction experts, a marvelous team of translators, and a group of 50 eager teenagers ready to take part in whatever labors the experts deemed necessary. I was merely a supervisor charged with ensuring the project was completed safely, on time, and hopefully with high morale.

Don't Run... Use Your Words

Each morning, I had a meeting with my talented team of translators. They really were a lifeline and I can't imagine what it would have been like to try to complete the project without them. At our meeting I would assign each one of my five Slovak-speaking coworkers various tasks for the day. This ranged from seeking additional extension cords for power tools to renegotiating storage space in the school gymnasium. We were a well-oiled machine and my team accomplished everything I gave them, gleefully and speedily.

About midway through the week, I felt my team was getting along so well we could try operating at a more casual, informal, friendly level. As I assigned tasks for the day, I threw in one or two off-the-wall and over-the-top ridiculous chores – just to lighten the mood. After asking one translator to try and find some more saw blades, I added a request to also find some dynamite or other form of explosives as it would save us time digging holes. Martin, the recipient of said instruction, grinned uneasily in response to my request and subsequent witty smile. He gets me. Or so I thought. The next day I threw in a request to Katka to find an elephant for our big ribbon-cutting celebration. I cheekily explained I wanted a gimmick that would really stand out and give the whole event a carnival-like feel. Just as Martin had the day before, Katka smiled at my odd request. I was bonding with my Slovak friends. Or so I thought.

The next day, Katka began the meeting by informing me that while she had tracked down an elephant in the Bratislava zoo, they were unwilling to lend the animal out for private functions. I loved that she was playing along with me. I joked with Katka that I was disappointed, and she should at least find me something magnificent to ride around on if she wasn't able to procure an elephant. Martin chimed in, explaining that using explosives would require a permit, and was not allowed on school grounds anyway. "Excuses, excuses..." I responded wryly. I was bonding with my Slovak friends. Or so I thought.

On the final day of our project, I was awakened by a knock at my door far earlier than I would have liked. As I opened it, there stood Martin clearly excited about something. He hurriedly explained he'd managed to find a type of explosive that would be allowed on school grounds. I rubbed my eyes and tried to grasp what on earth he was talking about. Before I could even form a question, we were in a van driving away. Martin was rambling on about how we had to pay a Russian guy he knew for explosives and this was not the kind of guy you wanted to keep waiting. The van stopped in a dark alley in a town nearby. As Martin stepped out of the vehicle, he told me to give him a significant amount of cash. Seeing the panic in his eyes, I did. He left me in the van and disappeared into the darkness only to emerge a few minutes later balancing a collection of large boxes while speed-walking toward the van.

He threw the boxes in and we sped away. "What just happened?" I asked, clinging onto my seat in terror as we sped through winding streets. The sun began to rise.

"Take a look!" Martin responded gleefully, clearly energized by all the excitement that had just taken place. I leaned into the back seat and opened one of the

Don't Run... Use Your Words

boxes. It was filled with fireworks. Rockets in a myriad of shapes and sizes were jammed into each of the boxes. It suddenly hit me that Martin had taken my bizarre and nonsensical request seriously. He had been searching for something explosive and also legal with the same fervor he'd displayed in accomplishing all the actual and useful tasks I'd assigned him. I wasn't sure what to do... I had just procured a sizable amount of fireworks and felt the only way to recognize Martin's bravery and efforts was to actually use them. So that's what I decided to do; I would indeed add a carnival-like flare to our playground's grand opening. At the worksite later that morning, I told my construction managers about our stock of pyrotechnics. I asked them to set the fireworks up on a hill a safe distance from the playground and keep the whole thing a secret. I was hoping to pull off this stunt during the excitement of the ribbon cutting without my bosses knowing I had anything to do with it.

Our hard-working students arrived and were busy making last minute preparations for the big celebration when one student came running into my office, panting and excited. "I can't believe you're actually going to pull this off! This is going to be epic!" he exclaimed.

"What are you talking about?" I retorted, guessing that he'd somehow found out about the fireworks. "Well, don't tell anyone, it's meant to be a surprise," I pleaded.

"It's kind of hard to keep as a surprise," he said. "It just pooped near the slide." Shock and a bit of alarm struck me. Who had just pooped near the slide? What was this kid talking about? I immediately made my way out to the playground we had just finished. It was now covered in balloons and streamers and waiting to be played on for the first time.

There, amidst the colors and bunting, stood a massive gleaming white horse. I was not amused. Horses and I generally do not get along. I hate to say it, but they seem like pretentious creatures. They look down at you down from long noses as if to say, "That's right, I'm important. People tend to me constantly and I cost a fortune." I just don't get along with them. One tried to run me off into the desert in Egypt and kill me – admittedly I've been a little bitter ever since.

I strode onto the playground demanding to know what this pretentious monstrosity was doing on my work site. There, standing beside it and brimming with pride, was Katka, my faithful translator. "You said to find something magnificent to ride on. We may not have an elephant, but we do have a stallion." I didn't know what to say. As gently as possible I tried to explain that a worksite soon to be teeming with hundreds of small children really was not the ideal place for a massive horse. Katka flared with intensity and explained she had gone through a lot of effort to bring this 'beautiful creature' and expected me not only to admire it, but to ride on it triumphantly during the ceremony.

Though I adamantly protested, Katka and the crowd of students and leaders now assembled were not going to release me from this fate. Before I knew it, small children were beginning to gather around the playground. Teachers, parents, and visitors from the town assembled in front of a giant ribbon strung across the front of the slide. You could see in the eyes of the gathered children the eagerness to be unleashed on this new toy, so tantalizingly close. All that stood between them and hours of amusement was a thin ribbon and a very uncomfortable-looking man on a horse.

I wanted to be off the horse about as much as those children wanted to be on the playground. The principal of the school approached, rather amused at the sight of me struggling to maintain control over a very strong and jittery beast. He said a few words, after which I was supposed to say a few words. Then we would cut the ribbon; the children could play, I could dismount, and the fireworks would begin. My construction leaders had been told to begin preparing the fireworks when the principal's speech ended. That way they would go off as I finished speaking right as the ribbon was cut, producing a magical culminating moment of excitement.

That was the plan. But as the principal spoke, it became clear he was announcing some sort of surprise that delighted the Slovak-speaking crowd and drew gasps from my translators. This was definitely not in the script. Just as Katka tried to explain to me what was being said, I looked up to see the film crew from our base camp alongside what appeared to be a TV crew and a small crowd of important-looking people making their way toward us. I struggled to calm the diabolical monster of a horse I was perched upon, while Katka explained that the city mayor was making a surprise appearance to thank us in person. This was indeed an honor, but a badly timed one.

The mayor stood next to the principal who whispered in his ear and pointed to me. The mayor took the microphone and began to speak to the crowd. Katka came forward and translated his speech. He was thanking our team for all of our hard work and inviting us to visit any time we'd like. He finished his address to the crowd and turned to try and shake my hand. The horse was already nervous at having to stand in front of a crowd of people and was very uncooperative. I awkwardly tried to grab the mayor's hand to return his gesture but the horse danced about, making contact between us impossible.

I nearly had his hand when a sudden 'BOOM!' sounded above us. Sparkles in a rainbow of colors spread out across the sky. The fireworks had been set off. My psychotic stallion bucked and took off running around the playground in response. Children leapt onto the new playground (which cleared a path for the horse to continue its haphazard route) and the mayor darted out of the way of the charging steed. Katka raced after me trying to rescue me from the beast's rampage. All the while, flashes of light and thunderous explosions went off overhead.

The whole scene was complete chaos. I know this because the cameras caught the whole thing, and I later watched it unfold in magnificent mayhem on a TV screen together with my bosses. The lesson from this whole ordeal was very clear to me: humor doesn't always translate perfectly into other cultures. CCKs, in particular, benefit from having to communicate across a wider variety of linguistic and cultural divides as part of the experience of growing up. It's not always easy and it may not necessarily feel like a benefit, but these experiences sharpen skills that are ever more important in an increasingly globalized world.

I've met many fellow TCKs who recall how difficult it was learning a new language, a new set of gestures, new slang terms, a new accent, or a new style of etiquette. It can seem unfair – many people grow up and get to use the same language, etc., their whole lives. Why should we have to adapt so much? The truth of the matter is that most people will have to pick up additional communication styles. The world is ever-more connected, and being able to function across cultures is becoming less and less a nice advantage and more and more an absolute necessity. It's far easier to learn these skills while you're young and far harder for adults to pick up new skills. Many who didn't get the opportunity to do so in their youth struggle to do so later in life.

My friends, don't take the hard-earned ability to communicate for granted. Thanks to technology and other social trends, the ability to express and take in thoughts in a face-to-face context is growing more valuable and rare. A recent poll found that 39% of Americans spend more time socializing online than face-to-face.[6] Some government bodies are already worried that using social media has reduced the vocabulary of teenagers to the point that they may struggle to gain meaningful employment.[7] Communicating effectively is becoming a prized commodity. No matter how smart you are or what other skills you have, the ability to communicate, listen, and even resolve conflict will help connect your intellect and your skills to the world around you.

If you like lists, this part's for you:

* *'Some TCKs never learn to deal with conflict because they know if they simply outwait the situation, or ignore it, they or the other person or persons will be gone. Then no one has to 'worry about it' anymore. This does not serve well in adulthood where conflict management in careers as well as home is a needed skill.'*[2]

* *'Conflicts are a normal and natural part of everyone's life. Conflicts are simply the disputes and disagreements that occur between two people. While we tend to think of conflict only in terms of its negative effects, the fact is that conflict can also be positive. Without conflict there is no growth or progress.'*[3]

* Helping mediate other people's conflict can help highlight skills you can use yourself. Additionally, remember to be aware of the **story, feelings**, and **identities** behind the situation: don't underestimate the importance of context in a conflict.[4]

* Empathy is essential in being able to resolve conflict and is, unfortunately, on the decline.[5] Vulnerability can help preserve a connection for empathy in a relationship.

* It's much harder to maintain a sense of empathy through online communication.

* Because of frequent cultural transitions (and often through trial and error or observation), TCKs tend

to have a broader pallet of communication styles to draw from. This is an increasingly useful if not essential ability in an ever-globalizing world – and worth intentionally focusing on.

---

[1] *Third Culture Kids, The Experience of Growing Up Among Worlds*. David C. Pollock and Ruth E. Van Reken. Nicholas Brealey America; Revised Edition. 2009.

[2] *Belonging Everywhere & Nowhere: Insights into Counseling the Globally Mobile*. Lois J. Bushong, M.S. Mango Tree Intercultural Services. 2013.

[3] *Emotional Resilience and the Expat Child*. Julia Simens. Summertime. 2011.

[4] *The Global Nomad's Guide to University Transition*. Tina Quick. Summertime. 2010.

[5] *The Empathy Deficit*. David C. Keith O'Brien. 2010. (Excerpt from *The Boston Globe*). http://www.boston.com/bostonglobe/ideas/articles/2010/10/17/the_empathy_deficit/?s_campaign=8315

[6] *Generation Lonely?* Badoo. 2012. http://mashable.com/2012/06/14/social-media-real-world-infographic/

[7] *Teenagers 'only use 800 different words a day'*. Aislinn Laing. 2010. (Excerpt from *The Daily* Telegraph). http://mashable.com/2012/06/14/social-media-real-world-infographic/

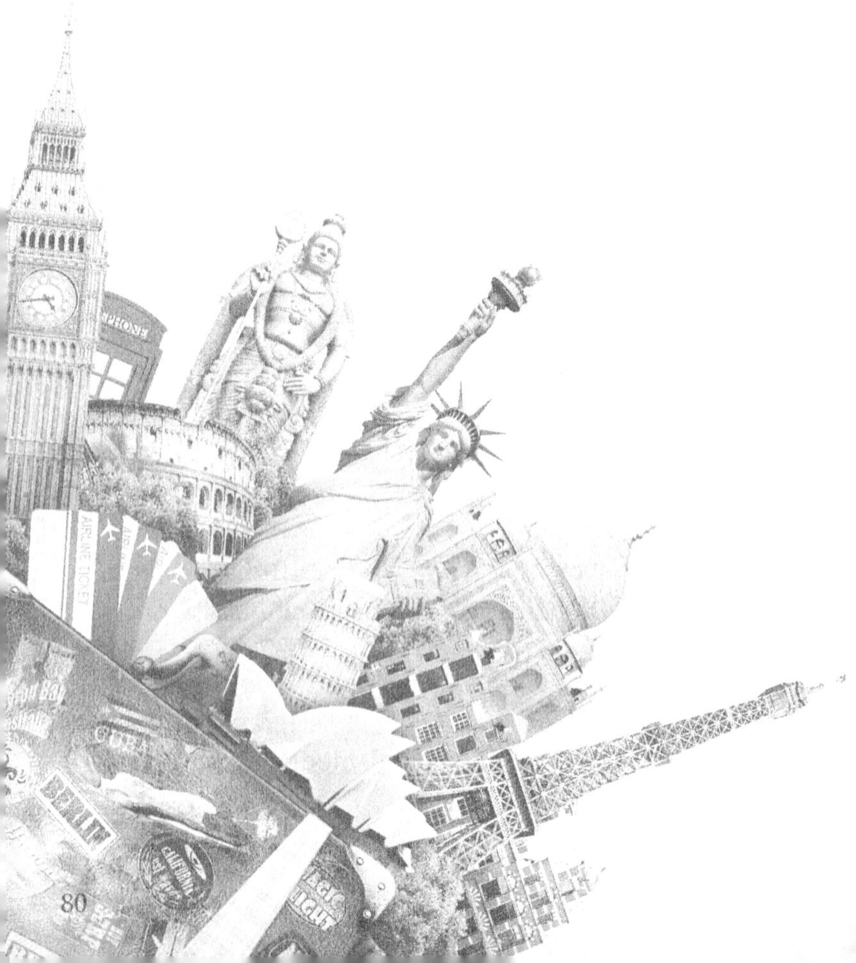

CHAPTER 4

Air Raid Sirens and Gangster Rap

Confidence in Change

I was still working in Europe when my parents decided to move to the U.S. permanently. I'd only really been to the U.S. for brief trips since my childhood there and I was excited at the thought of being able to visit them and hear of their findings. On one trip over, I made a startling discovery that tested my ability to appreciate change. Ultimately, however, it did help broaden my perspectives.

It was a warm morning in Pennsylvania. I thought it was a beautiful place, and was glad to see my parents happy there. I awoke to the sun shining gloriously through the windows, the scent of grass wafting through the air, the birds chirping. All I needed to complete the feeling of utter contentment was a cup of tea. I headed downstairs to join Mom and Dad who were already at the kitchen table chatting over morning beverages. You could feel the relaxation in the air. It was as if nature had slowed down so everyone could stop and take a breath, smell the roses, hear the rustling of leaves and the laughter of children. You get the idea.

I sat, taking it all in over a nice cup of tea. Suddenly, the idyllic mood was shattered by the rising whine of an air raid siren. My picturesque morning was unexpectedly under attack! Alarmed, I put down my tea and began to scramble for... I don't know what. I didn't know what to do. I had lived in places where that sound really did mean impending danger. In those places I was well versed in how to react to such a warning. Here in my parents' house, I was desperately unprepared.

Dive under the table – that seemed like a reasonable course of action. As I began to scurry under the table amidst the blaring warning signal outside, I caught sight of Mom and Dad. They seemed completely unaware of anything out of the ordinary. They were still sipping their coffee as if nothing was happening; as if our lives were in no way in any danger, as if the air raid sirens were signaling the sale of sweets or ice-cream on the street, rather than the possibility of impending doom.

My parents had now noticed my panicked expression and my move toward the safety found beneath their kitchen table. We all paused, staring at each other with confusion, all the while the sirens wailed outside. I didn't understand why they were not joining me in seeking cover – they did not understand why I was acting like a paranoid lunatic at the breakfast table. This standoff finally ended when I asked them the obvious question: why were air raid sirens blaring outside and what should we be doing in response?

Mom and Dad burst into laughter. This made me feel more than a little embarrassed. They explained the sirens were to alert the volunteer firefighters of the town to muster in response to a fire. So the sirens *were* an indication of alert, just not necessarily wide-spread danger as I had anticipated. This explanation, however, only led to more questions from me. For a start, I was unfamiliar with the idea of *volunteer* firefighters. Everywhere I had lived previously employed systems involving full-time firefighters either provided by the military or by the government of whatever locality I was living in. The idea of volunteers was fine if it were in connection to some sort of charity. But volunteers were inherently optional participants. That's the whole point

– volunteering for something is a choice, not a mandate.

I was desperately uncomfortable with the idea that my parents' safety was in the hands of volunteers. Don't get me wrong, volunteers are great, but something as important as firefighting should surely be a full-time duty. What if a fire breaks out and all the volunteers are busy with their actual jobs and can't get away in time to attend their *voluntary* life-saving activities? Based on the experiences and understanding gained from where I'd lived, this just seemed like madness to me. I conveyed my concern to my parents who looked to be rather calm at the prospect of entrusting their potential rescue to volunteers with other careers and commitments. They suggested I speak with the volunteer firefighters myself and told me about a steak cookout fundraiser being held that very weekend to raise money for the fire station. I could ask my questions there. So, not only were volunteers entrusted with the safety of the town, but they also had to hold charity events to get the equipment they needed? This whole situation had elevated itself a step closer to insanity as far as I was concerned.

That weekend, I did attend the fire station fundraiser, and was fortunate enough to meet one of the volunteers in charge of the station. He offered me a tour. I leapt at the opportunity and later that week was shown around the surprisingly modern and well-equipped station in my parents' town. As politely as possible, I asked him to explain to me how the whole volunteer system worked, especially if the entire mechanism was dependent on the generosity of the town and the willingness of volunteers to put themselves in harm's way while also maintaining other jobs.

What I found out surprised and impressed me. The fire station in my parents' small town had better response times than the national average, very modern equipment, and a healthy roster of volunteers. The fundraisers were always well attended and adequately provided for the needs of the station. The whole system functioned incredibly well. In fact, the voluntary nature of it provided a focal point for the community. Fundraisers weren't just an opportunity to cover expenses, they were a common meeting point for the whole town. After all, everyone had an interest in the fire department that kept them safe. It was a way for everyone to socialize and strengthen community bonds. It was a benefit I hadn't seen as much in the systems I was used to.

Experiencing different sides

Looking back, I realize my initial concerns arose out of my only being exposed to a socialized setup where it was the government's responsibility to provide for essential needs like safety. The area my parents relocated to had a far more independent solution to some of those needs. Arguments about how far reaching a government should be in its provision for the needs of its people, or how much freedom it should allow them in meeting those needs, rage across the world. Political parties are formed on the basis of such questions and lots of debates with people screaming, yelling, and every now and then throwing things are rooted in determining this balance. I am not in a position to advocate one system is better than the other. I think different systems serve different people.

What I do know is that I am sincerely grateful I learned to appreciate a way of doing things different from what I am accustomed to. I believe I have some of my TCK-ness to thank for that. Perhaps it sounds obvious, but being able to understand – even appreciate – that not everyone does things the way you do, or the way you're used to, is an impressive skill. Many problems around the globe arise from an inability to understand where the line is drawn on whether an idea is a universal standard (like human rights) or simply a different system to meet the needs of different people with different values and priorities.

Having grown up with strong influence from both the U.S. and the U.K., I often have to try to explain one group to the other. I am fortunate enough to have attended school in both systems, and as a result got to witness firsthand how differently two countries or groups of people can see the same events. The very circumstances which brought the United States into existence are a great example of this variance in perspective. I remember being taught in the U.S. that the founding fathers took a stand against British tyranny and oppression, seizing the opportunity to create a nation and society based on noble principles and freedom. In the U.K., I recall a lot more emphasis on how Britain invested heavily in settling the New World only to have it stolen by opportunistic insurrectionists. Thankfully, we all get along now.

Having been taught both sides of the story (or at least both interpretations of the story) I appreciate that one side is not necessarily right and the other wrong.

It's more that both sides interpret the events through separate sets of lenses shaped by different values and beliefs. Around the world, language, culture, history, tradition, values, and priorities come together to form unique blends that define places and the people who live in them. As TCKs and CCKs, we have the amazing opportunity to stroll through these unique blends.

Of course, in reality, we do more than stroll through different systems. We engage them. Maybe not always willingly at first, but eventually, and usually out of necessity, we do. *'TCKs don't simply study other cultures, they experience them by living in them.'*[1] We must adapt to the many environments we are a part of. We are affected by change, and *everything* is constantly changing. Some things are changing slowly, some things rapidly. Even the things we think are stable are usually just changing very gradually. Huge majestic mountains that seem eternal and make for great skiing are just growing or shrinking at an imperceptible rate... unless they are volcanoes. Then they have a tendency to change rapidly, suddenly, and violently and are not so ideal for skiing.

TCKs are usually a bit more accustomed to the volcanic rate of change. Moving to a new home in a new country or culture may take months of preparation, but in the short span of a plane ride, everything changes. TCKs tend to be pretty good at being flexible and adapting to new surroundings. We might not always enjoy it, we might not always want it, but out of necessity, most of us have learned to deal with change at this pace. Even TCKs who don't move often but live in an international environment must deal with the swift turnover of people around them. If everyone around you is constantly moving, you're still dealing with a rapid rate of change.[2]

CHANGE MANAGEMENT

Learning to deal with change – and learning to do it well – are incredibly valuable skills. An article from the BBC goes so far as to say that our ability to embrace change may be the key to happiness.[3] One interpretation of this would conclude that TCKs should be some of the world's happiest people. I've certainly felt the thrill of arriving in a new place; starting fresh, learning new things, meeting new people, reinventing myself as an improved version on the last. Change really can be energizing, refreshing – invigorating even. That being said, I don't always feel the positive side of change. I know plenty of fellow TCKs who feel exhausted by the rate of change they must live in. Many people yearn for stability. As much as I have enjoyed change and the freshness it brings to my life, I have also mourned the things I've lost because of it, and wished for more time with people I've had to leave or been left by.

Change is inevitable, and it's going to bring both positive and negative effects. Ideally, the best we can do is capitalize on the good and learn to overcome the bad. That may sound simplistic, but as humans we will go to great lengths to avoid that simplicity, instead expending a lot of thought and effort trying to halt the sometimes swift, sometimes lethargic, but ever-constant march of change. The inability to accept change has some fairly significant effects on a person, and in some ways highlights the great strength many TCKs don't even realize they have in dealing with change.

For instance, the way we look at other people is influenced by how we deal with change. Let's say you're walking down the street and you pass by a homeless person asking for money. The way you perceive them could be linked very strongly to how well you deal with change. If you accept change, are comfortable with it, and deal with it well, you're more likely to see that person asking for money as more than who they are now. You're not going to see them just as a homeless person needing money and making you feel guilty, sad, or even annoyed. Being familiar with change means you can look at that person and know they have not always been what they are now. You're more likely to wonder about that homeless person's past: how did they get where they are now? In essence, you're able to appreciate the power of story. Everyone has one, and change is what moves our stories along.

Accepting change also means we see the potential in the future. Change has brought us to where we are, and we won't be staying here. Change will propel us forward – willingly or not. This means an appreciation for change could be strongly linked to characteristics such as generosity, charity, and compassion.[3] If we can't see a future for the homeless person on the street, and if they're stuck in our minds as forever being the homeless person, then why help? But if we see them as someone who came from something and is on the way to something, we're far more likely to be willing to invest in where they're going. We're more likely to believe in positive change, a better future.

An inability to accept change would pit us against an unstoppable force. We cannot control everything.

This is a fact of life everyone must deal with. Again, for TCKs the pace may be quickened, but it is a universal fact. We're all going to age, we're all going to change, and plenty of the circumstances that affect us are simply out of our control. I'm not saying to give up on everything and just go with the flow, entirely. There are things we do have control over, like our perceptions and the impact we can have on those around us. But I think one of the healthiest things TCKs can do is learn to appreciate the balance of controllable and uncontrollable circumstances in life.

Having to deal with a lot of change allows us to have wider perspectives on things. We see situations, people, and circumstances from varying angles because we're in motion, too. It certainly doesn't always come easily, but don't underestimate how incredibly valuable a broad perspective is in an increasingly multicultural, globalizing world... TCKs are useful.

Embrace It

In adapting to new environments and surroundings, TCKs must collect the cultural information around them. This sounds obvious, but it's not a natural skill for everyone. I've traveled with people who are unable to hear the symphony of their surroundings because they're singing their own tune at the tops of their lungs. All too often I've witnessed people unwilling to take in the culture around them in a new or foreign place. Though it may be out of defense or fear, they compensate by blasting their own culture at high volume. A friend of mine visiting from the U.S.

immediately and loudly dismissed Euro bank notes as "silly fake-looking money" because they were different colors and sizes. (U.S. currency is all the same size and roughly the same color.) As a result, every time we needed to pay for something, he'd just hand me a wad of money and tell me to deal with it. He was unwilling to even take the time to learn the denominations of the money, let alone the exchange rate. I tried explaining to him that the notes were different colors and sizes in order to assist blind or sight-impaired people. He didn't care. It wasn't what he was used to, and it was, therefore, automatically inferior.

There was a professor in my university who felt very passionate about music. He wasn't actually a professor of music, in fact my degree was in youth, community work, and applied theology. But he was a good professor: very wise, very old, very friendly. He was one of those people who was so clever when it came to academia that his energy for it seemed to have been siphoned from more mundane tasks (like getting dressed or remembering where to be and when). He often had mismatched socks, misaligned buttons on his shirt, and a matted mess of hair just begging for a family of small birds to take up residence. But he was brilliant. Every now and then he would completely forget which class he was lecturing to and deliver very insightful teaching to us... about something completely different than what we were actually there for. For the most part we didn't mind because he was one of the most engaging teachers I've ever met. His love of music was part of what fueled his charm. He may have been an old, badly dressed professor, but he was an expert in pop music, rap music, gangster rap, and even some death metal. People his age, in his profession, from his part of the world traditionally would listen to classical music and opera (one would assume). While I'm sure he did so as well, he also seemed to know every word to every rap song ever written. The marvelous thing about this knowledge was that he applied it to his lessons.

He may have been lecturing on deontological ethical theory, but he could somehow pull in words from seemingly unrelated genres of music to illustrate his point. We loved it. We'd sit hanging on every word waiting for that magic moment when he would, in his marvelously academic posh English accent, utter a phrase like, "*'Me and my partner, in my Impala, poppin' on collars, tossing up dollars...*'[4] in many ways this outlines the beginning of the artist's diatribe against traditional models of socio-economic progression based on an antiquated hierarchical system rooted in..." It was magical. You just haven't lived until you've heard a learned man of academia say, "poppin' on collars, tossing up dollars" in a proper English accent. Higher education is fun.

I don't really think my professor recreationally listened to gangster rap. Well, maybe he did. It's a fantastic image, picturing him at home in a quaint English cottage, sitting with a cup of tea in a large cushioned chair next to a pleasantly crackling fire in an ornate fireplace, wearing a smoking jacket and blaring bass-heavy rhymes at an obscene volume, bopping his head to the beat, wisps of untamed gray hair rhythmically swaying as he sings along, all the while reading the Sunday newspaper. In reality, it's not a style of music that would occur in his native, natural habitat or peer group. It would have taken some effort on his part to actually find and listen to that particular style of music. And he wouldn't have been able to quote it in lectures unless he made room in his life to hear it. I think culture works the same way.

As we move into different cultures, we have to make room for them in our lives. Intentionally engaging with new cultures adds aspects of them to our lives. Some of my music-loving professor's unique charm stemmed from his open-mindedness and willingness to add aspects of a unique musical genre to his repertoire of understanding. We don't replace the old catalogue of cultures and traditions we've collected, we add to it. As TCKs, in order to thrive in new surroundings, we have to be able to increase our own cultural repertoires – otherwise we risk feeling like nothing more than visitors in our own lives.

Cultural consistency

As TCKs, we may gain a better chance at open-mindedness simply from becoming cultural observers and adopters by necessity. We wouldn't last long in a new country if, for example, we refused to use their local currency – clinging stubbornly instead to whatever money we're used to and expecting everyone around us to adapt to our system. As another example, in Thailand, they drive on the left-hand side of the road (quite a few countries do: 75 in total, according to Wikipedia), even though most countries around them drive on the right-hand side. Obviously, if someone were to arrive in Thailand, get into a car, and drive away from the airport on the right side of the road – into oncoming traffic – they would cause rather a lot of upset, inconvenience, panic, and general confusion. Once apprehended, the excuse that they were merely acting according to the customs held by their previous location (the driving on the right part, not the driving into oncoming traffic part), would be disregarded. They would most definitely be considered in the wrong, legally and otherwise.

That may seem obvious, but infractions of this nature happen all the time. Not only do people drive on the left in Thailand, pedestrian traffic also keeps to the left. So if you're coming up a flight of stairs from the metro, you'd be expected to do so on the left side of the corridor. Yet, without fail on journeys to Thailand (and other left-preferring nations) visitors and tourists can be seen fighting their way up stairs through oncoming pedestrians on the right side, carrying a look of annoyance. I doubt those going against the flow are doing so to mark some deeply rooted objection, it's just that they haven't taken the time to observe that the system around them is different from *their* version of normal.

TCKs really cannot afford the luxury of refusing to take the time to observe and adapt to the systems around them. It's one thing to suffer the annoyance of constantly going against the flow as a visitor, unable to adapt. But to live your whole life that way would be exhausting and deeply alienating. Pedestrian patterns, etiquette while eating, greeting, or leaving, as well as countless other customs and traditions mankind engages in on a daily basis are not universal. They vary country to country, region to region. TCKs often face the daunting task of not only learning a new way of doing things, but also having to maintain previous ways of doing things. If you're a German family living in Japan, you would most likely interact with your family as you always have – in a German fashion, while also adding local Japanese practices to your repertoire for outside the home.

As a result, most TCKs knowingly or intuitively enter into a phase of observation when they arrive at a new 'home.' *'TCKs are like cultural chameleons – they wait and watch to determine which cultural color they must turn into in order to fit in.'*[5] Often fueled by the sting of being the outsider and embarrassing oneself by not behaving according to the local standard, TCKs can seem withdrawn or noncommittal during this phase. As I mentioned previously, while I learned an American accent during my early years in Las Vegas, I was perceived as a very quiet boy at school. I wasn't generally a quiet person, I was just devoting my time to listening so I could adapt.

'Successful interactions with other cultures come from an open mind, knowledge and experience.'[6] Arriving in a new place and focusing on observing with an open mind helps you process your observations positively and constructively. Tina Quick suggests looking through a travel guide before you arrive to help get an overview and build some knowledge about where you're heading.[5] Finally, you've got to experience a culture in order to adapt to it well. Don't be afraid to interact: taste the food, meet the people, try to learn at least some of the language. Mistakes will be made, but a hearty apology and a sincere desire to learn go a long way.

In her book, *Subtle Differences, Big Faux Pas*, Elizabeth Vennekens-Kelly draws attention to the difference between 'high context' communication where more indirect approaches and suggestions are used to convey thoughts and feelings (Japanese culture tends to be more 'high context'), and 'low context' communication which uses far more direct means and style (U.S. culture tends to be more 'low context'). It's a good idea to bear in mind which style you're more comfortable with and which style you'll be living amongst. Elizabeth also addresses several areas that commonly cause difficulty when learning to interact with a new culture. Things to look out for include physical contact, appropriate gestures, views on timeliness, table manners, topics for polite conversation vs. topics off limits, style of dress, and even local superstitions.[6]

SELF-RELIANCE

One side effect that having to repeatedly adapt to new places can cause in TCKs is a tendency toward self-reliance. It's nearly impossible to systematically teach someone all the nuances necessary to blend into a local culture. Many things must be personally learned and experienced. While the very nature of learning to adapt to those around you requires *those around you* (other people), TCKs must often rely on their own strength and individual drive to consciously or unconsciously adjust their behavior. Obviously, peer pressure and group influence can affect some aspects, but the more subtle details often require personal determination to change. As one TCK put it, *'The only person who could really decide to make a place a home was me, I couldn't keep waiting for other people to do it for me, and I had to make the conscious decision for myself to be fully a part of a place.*[7] This is also why TCKs really need to be secure in their sense of core identity. Aspects of how you interact with your environment can change, but who you really are deep down, should not.

Self-reliance can also be fueled by the ongoing and often repeated transition that happens when the shift is made from 'us' to 'them' to 'us'. Usually when a person leaves a group, a place, a school, or a country, they do so having established some kind of feeling of 'us'. You're familiar with your friends, you feel some degree of belonging in the community, and you have some degree of familiarity with the customs of the people around you even if you don't have a 'complete' sense of belonging. Leaving that, you arrive somewhere new and the people around you are new, they're 'them' – different from you. Adapting, learning, and building a sense of belonging will hopefully shift the new group you're a part of to becoming 'us' as well. But the common denominator factored into both 'them' and 'us' is you. Just you. As TCKs, we are more prone to be self-reliant because there is usually not much else in our lives that can maintain the same degree of consistency as ourselves.

In light of this, it's important to be able to balance self-reliance with some healthy interdependence. It seems (in my experience at least) that we human beings sometimes really like easily categorized, black-and-white extremes. It may be simpler that way, but it is not necessarily accurate. Just because one person has let you down doesn't mean everyone will. Just because some people have faded from your life doesn't mean everyone will. There have been times when the feelings of isolation that come with being the new person, and the sting of being alone, have pushed me to believe I must shield myself from the inevitable disappointment that comes from trusting other people. I convince myself I am destined to plow through life strong, noble, and alone.

In reality, we're not built for that. *'We are made as relational beings and when we attempt to live a life that is not relational, things can derail in our lives.'*[1] It's also not a very efficient way of functioning. If we indulge the 'I'm alone, it's me against the world' defenses early on, we can easily become micromanagers, ineffectual martyrs, and people incapable of delegating. Delegation and teamwork are essential for just about every aspect of life. Alone, one can only accomplish so much; working together we are capable of incredibly impressive things. This isn't to say we should open our hearts with reckless abandon – some people are not dependable and it's a wise practice to discern who is trustworthy and who is not. But finding balance through depending on people and being dependable yourself is immensely valuable. Growing up in transience with an ability to adapt and deal with change may take some extra effort, but it adds to the myriad of reasons that well-adjusted TCKs are a very powerful ingredient in making the world a better place. Change is happening all the time. We can't stop it, so we may as well harness it to accomplish some good – for us and for the world around us.

If you like lists, this part's for you:

* Being able to understand, and even appreciate, that not everyone does things the way you do, or the way you're used to, is an impressive and useful skill. Because TCKs often experience many cultures, they tend to have a wider worldview.

* How you deal with change has a big effect on how you see the world. An ability to embrace change and deal with it well gives you appreciation for both your 'story' and others' as well.

* As we move into different cultures, we have to make room for them in our lives. *'Successful interactions with other cultures come from an open mind, knowledge and experience.'*[6]

* Repeated adaptation and transition often leads to TCKs being very self-reliant. It's a valuable skill, but should be tempered with the ability to connect with and depend on others too. *'We are made as relational beings and when we attempt to live a life that is not relational, things can derail in our lives.'*[1]

---

[1] *Belonging Everywhere & Nowhere: Insights into Counseling the Globally Mobile.* Lois J. Bushong, M.S. Mango Tree Intercultural Services. 2013.

[2] *Third Culture Kids, The Experience of Growing Up Among Worlds.* David C. Pollock and Ruth E. Van Reken. Nicholas Brealey America; Revised Edition. 2009.

[3] *A Point of View: Why embracing change is the key to happiness.* AL Kennedy. 2013.
(Excerpt from *BBC News Magazine*).
http://www.bbc.co.uk/news/magazine-23986212

[4] *Snoop Dogg*. Snoop Dogg. 2000. (From the album, *The Last Meal*).

[5] *The Global Nomad's Guide to University Transition.* Tina Quick. Summertime. 2010.

[6] *Subtle Differences, Big Faux Pas.* Elizabeth Vennekens-Kelly. Summertime. 2012.

[7] *The Worlds Within – An anthology of TCK art and writing: young, global and between cultures.* Summertime. 2014.

CHAPTER 5

Live in the Now, but Don't Get Kidnapped

Restlessness, rootlessness, and preparing for the future

With my parents settling into life in the United States, I continued gallivanting on the other side of the Atlantic and eventually moved to Turkey for a job working with youth on a U.S. Air Force base. I thoroughly enjoyed living there, but soon realized the part of Turkey I was living in was less easy to travel from than Western Europe. Before too long, I felt the call of wanderlust. I had to travel. Exploring somewhere new became a need. I'd recently seen something in *National Geographic* about ancient monasteries in Armenia and as that was roughly in my part of the world, it was clearly meant to be.

Conveniently, I have a good friend named Walter who lived near me in Turkey at the time. Walter has the charming propensity to say 'yes' to just about anything when it comes to travel. Often Walter agrees to an adventure before I've had time to explain what exactly we'll be embarking on.

"Walter, I think we should –"

"Yes."

"But it involves wearing –"

"I'm on it."

"We'll have to eat –"

"Sounds great."

"We'll need to buy –"

"I already own two."

So Walter and I rented a car, loaded it with junk food, and set out from Southern Turkey for Armenia by way of Georgia. From the start, it was destined to be a fly-by-the-seat-of-your-pants adventure. We didn't have a roadmap or a GPS and the stereo in the car wouldn't work. We were confident enough in our old-school navigational abilities to make it without a GPS, and we thought we could just stop at a gas station to get a map. The lack of music, however, very nearly cancelled the whole endeavor.

As it turned out, it was far more difficult than we thought to find a road map of Eastern Turkey. To this day I believe only a handful are actually in existence. Using a compass, we just pointed ourselves in the right direction and tried to pick roads which seemed to match that heading. We'd stopped at quite a few gas stations before reaching one that had a map. It was proudly displayed behind protective glass – truly we were in the presence of a rare artifact. Walter and I did our best to sketch a copy of the roads we would need and the names of places along the way. All the while we were closely watched by a cashier who seemed ready to leap on us should we make any threatening gestures toward the sacred map. Armed with a rudimentary sketch of roughly what roads would lead us to the Turkish-Georgian border, we arrived that evening after a full day of driving. We were relieved and ecstatic to be standing on the cusp of racking up a new country.

Not that we keep count…

We definitely keep count.

After having our passports stamped leaving Turkey, our delight was abruptly cut short. We were stopped in the no-man's-land between Turkey and Georgia by a uniformed guard shouting at us in a language we did not understand. I always try to learn at least basic phrases in a country's language before visiting – I think it's the polite thing to do – but being yelled at exponentially decreases my ability to recall the appropriate pleasantries. We stopped the car and tried to comply with the angry guard. Inconveniently, stopping the car seemed only to annoy him further, so we proceeded forward, grinning inanely at him. This caused an even larger outburst, culminating in the brandishing of his gun. He pointedly banged it on the car, signaling us to stop. We couldn't win. Finally (and I believe only moments before he actually exploded, littering the area around us with angry pieces of himself), he stormed off.

We didn't know what to do. Before we had time to think, he returned with another guard who spoke some English. He informed us we could not bring a car that had been registered in Turkey into Georgia without the proper documentation. We definitely didn't have that. We were pretty well-stocked in the junk food department, but had almost nothing in the way of paperwork. A beginner's mistake, I know – but this whole trip was dreamed up and executed in a rather spur-of-the-moment fashion. We were told we had no choice but to return to Turkey.

I was devastated. We'd driven across the country, had the privilege of gazing at one of the few maps of the region in existence, and now wouldn't even be able to enter Georgia? We re-crossed the border, and had our passports stamped back in – a visible symbol of defeat. We parked nearby and contemplated our options. It was then I noticed a man sitting outside a nearby building. He was an elderly gentleman and I got the impression, judging by the well-worn chair and collection of empty cans surrounding it, that he passed quite a bit of time sitting there, taking in the view.

Live in the Now, but Don't Get Kidnapped

I decided he would be the key to our success. I leapt from the vehicle and mustered a combination of my ridiculously limited Turkish vocabulary with my most expressive gesturing. I tried to convey to the man that we would pay him to watch our vehicle while we ventured across the border. I'm not entirely sure he understood what I was asking, but he gave the affirmative, "*Tamam, abi!*" That was good enough for me. We were leaving our only means of conveyance with a stranger a thousand kilometers from home as we crossed various international borders on foot – what could possibly go wrong? Walter and I were tipsy with wanderlust and clearly not thinking straight.

The adventure was back on! Walter and I hurriedly tried to decide how we were going to convert our only-barely-planned-road-trip into a completely-unplanned-hiking-adventure. We had to leave most of our supplies in the car, but decided underwear, Pringles, and Pop-Tarts would probably sustain us. Besides, we really weren't equipped to carry much more than that. We loaded up our scant stock of essentials and headed back through the border. The Turkish guard was amused to see us for a third time in less than an hour, but dutifully stamped us out... again.

This time we made it into Georgia. We quickly discovered we'd arrived quite late, which meant finding somewhere to stay was going to be a challenge. We had always planned on sleeping in the car, the lack of which was now going to add some complications to the remainder of our journey. The details are a bit blurry at this point, but I recall we managed to find a man who seemed to understand we needed shelter. He led us through a small, dark alley to a door and handed us a key before disappearing. Walter and I opened the door and found a very dark room. There were no lights and by now it was nighttime. Using only the lights on our watches we fumbled around to find flat, soft spots and fell asleep.

The next morning we awoke and headed to Tbilisi, Georgia's capital, by way of *marshrutkas* – shared taxis with the amazing ability to defy the laws of physics by jamming more people into their confined interiors than should be possible. We took in a brief tour of the city thanks to a very kind Georgian who spoke German about as well as I did (not very well), and his British friend who also spoke some Georgian. The German-speaking Georgian drove us at breakneck speed through the city pointing out various monuments and historical sites along the way, giving what seemed to be passionate and detailed explanations for each. The British man sat in the passenger seat and translated his monologues for us. I'm fairly sure the translation we received was an abbreviated version at best. After the German-speaking Georgian spent five minutes explaining the importance of Stalin's mother's tomb (which sits in a pantheon atop a hill overlooking the city), our British friend delivered the translation as, "So Stalin's mum is buried here. Apparently she wanted her son to be a priest, but instead he killed a load of people." There you have it.

After our briefly narrated tour of Tbilisi, we once again crammed into a *marshrutka* and headed toward Armenia. After a relatively short ride, we arrived at the border. In all the excitement of converting our driving tour to a pedestrian tour, I'd forgotten the border was going to be a bit of a challenge. Technically, visas were required to enter Armenia, but as it was a spur-of-the-moment adventure, we hadn't had the time to procure them in advance. I was banking on the legends and rumors I'd heard about being able to negotiate your way across the border.

As the *marshrutka* neared the checkpoint, our fellow riders began pulling out identity cards and documentation. This sounds mundane but was nothing short of a *Cirque du Soliel* act, being there were 32 of us in an 18-passenger van. The task of reaching into your pocket was a cooperative effort between you and the person sitting on you, not to mention the person sitting under you as well. Inevitably, several people were elbowed in the eye, but other than a few bruises and the shattering of anything resembling personal space boundaries, the whole maneuver was executed quite quickly. Amidst all this, Walter and I realized we were the only non-Georgian or non-Armenian passengers in the vehicle. Everyone else, it seemed, had noticed this too.

At the Georgian side of the border, everyone piled out of the vehicle and walked through, displaying various forms of identification. Walter and I took much longer than everyone else as we were the only ones using passports. I was quite nervous as we approached the Armenian checkpoint. They didn't look like they were messing around – uniforms and weapons abounded. Trying our best to look confident, Walter and I walked to the shack and presented our passports as if this were a routine operation. Their reaction confirmed it clearly was not.

I'm not saying individuals from far-flung countries have never crossed that particular border before, but it didn't seem to be a regular occurrence – and the ones that may have come before us probably were responsible enough to have gotten the necessary visas ahead of time. The guard flicked through my passport once, twice, and then in an irate tone asked me something I couldn't understand. I feebly tried to explain I couldn't speak Armenian, which caused him to repeat his question in a louder and more irate tone. Further apologies on my part only raised his level of irritation.

Moments before this man exploded before my very eyes, littering angry pieces of himself all around (two near-explosions on one trip!), another guard with a basic command of English intervened. He explained to us what we already knew to be true: we did not have visas. He proceeded to ask questions about our plans in Armenia – none of which we had answers for. Our 'plan' was simply to go see ancient monasteries and feel cool for having explored new foreign lands. But that doesn't sound very good on official paperwork. Luckily for us the guard (either intentionally because he took pity on us, or unintentionally because he was a naturally trusting border guard) kept answering his own questions. All we had to do was nod our heads vigorously.

"Where are you staying in Armenia? You are going to nice hotel in Yerevan? Perhaps Marriott? Yes, it is beautiful hotel."

"Who has arranged your visit? Probably student travel, yes?"

We obligingly nodded. After the easiest interrogation ever, we were rewarded with shiny new stickers in our passports and were permitted to enter

Live in the Now, but Don't Get Kidnapped

Armenia. Once past the checkpoint, we found our rather annoyed group of fellow-*marshrutka* passengers waiting for us. The driver was kind enough not to abandon us in the middle of nowhere at the border, but in doing so had delayed the passage of everyone else in the vehicle. We apologized as best we could and packed ourselves back in amongst our fellow riders. It's one thing to have to be in the presence of people who are clearly annoyed at you, it's another thing to have your body pressed against them on all sides.

A couple of bumpy hours later, the *marshrutka* deposited us at our destination: Alaverdi. We were the only people to get off there and we watched as the van rumbled off, leaving us alone. Evening was looming and once again we would need to find shelter for the night. Walter and I walked down the small road that led into town. Again, I'm not suggesting we were the only far-flung visitors to have set foot in Alaverdi, but it was immediately apparent from the stares of the locals that visitors like us were few and far between. Luckily, looking out-of-place as we did attracted the attention of someone willing to offer a room for the night.

After a surprisingly restful sleep, Walter and I awoke keen to accomplish our goal: ancient monasteries. These historical gems were to be found in the hills and mountains around nearby Haghpat. We asked our host what was the best way to reach these treasures and were told we needed a car; the monasteries were too high up and too spread out to reach by foot in any reasonable amount of time. Our host kindly wrote in Armenian (which uses a unique alphabet that is neither Latin nor Cyrillic) something along the lines of, "Please take us to the monasteries" in our notebook. We then displayed it to anyone we could around town for the rest of the morning.

Perhaps it was our presentation technique, but there weren't many people volunteering to chauffeur us on our quest. Finally, around noon, I approached an admittedly dodgy-looking man leaning against a car. He read our plea and nodded confidently, causing ash to fall like a stream of pepper from the limp cigarette hanging out of the side of his mouth. Walter, who cannot often be accused of possessing the voice of reason, pulled me aside (which really wasn't necessary, our potential driver didn't speak a word of English) and pointed out that the man before us looked less than trustworthy.

"Nonsense!" I protested. "Beggars can't be choosers. He's willing to take us to the monasteries so I say we get in the car." At that, we hopped in. In hindsight: not a wise choice at all. On the way up the mountain, our driver took it upon himself to show us some of the sights of Alaverdi. There was a Soviet war memorial proudly displaying what I believe was a MiG-21 aircraft. Then there was the opportunity to sample a beverage I decided to call 'Frothy-Water'. It was dispensed from an aging machine of questionable cleanliness and had about a 50/50 froth to liquid ratio. It had no discernible taste. It was sort of like lightly carbonated water... but with froth. From there he took us to a perch on a cliff overlooking Alaverdi's most striking feature, the copper factory. Stretching from where we stood on the cliff down to the factory was a long cable, hanging from which was a contraption I affectionately dubbed the 'Cable-Car-of-Doom'. Our driver ushered us inside one of the rusted cable cars, grinning inanely. I stepped in gingerly, trying to look brave on the outside while being absolutely terrified on the inside. The instant I put my foot down in the aging carriage it groaned and sank nearly half a meter. I leapt in horror for solid ground and banged my head in the process. This delighted our driver immensely. Our relationship was not off to a good start.

Finally, we drove out of the town and up into the rising hills of Haghpat. It took a while – the roads were twisted, steep, and treacherous – but the view was stunning. As promised, a series of ancient monasteries were at the top, some with carvings and stonework dating back to the early centuries, not far removed from the days when Jesus Christ walked the earth. We even stumbled upon a priest who sang ancient prayers to us as we took in the history around us. Reaching your goal is satisfying. It's amazingly satisfying when your goal is a little far-fetched. It's unbelievably satisfying when your far-fetched goal surpasses your imagination. High in the remote hills of Armenia, my imagination was surpassed.

But the adventure wasn't over. As the sun began to set, Walter and I, filled with a profound sense of accomplishment and satisfaction, asked our driver to take us back to town. It was time to catch a *marshrutka* and begin our long trek home. By 'asked' I mean we repeated the word "*marshrutka*" loudly while pointing at our watches. It seemed to work. He started the car and Walter and I watched as the last of the monasteries faded into the distance below us... which was odd, because we needed to get down from the hills not go up further into them. I tapped our driver and once again pointed to my watch while mouthing as articulately as I could, "*marshrutka*". He said nothing, but continued up a steep road.

Walter and I began to grow concerned, and rightly so. None of our requests, protestations, or even panicked pleas stopped his ascent. Finally, on the edge of a cliff, he stopped, turned, and gave the international hand signal for 'pay me'. An uneasy feeling washed over me as I reached for my wallet. I realized the uneasy feeling was due to the fact that I was now breaking – and had been breaking for a while – *every* rule for safety I could think of in these situations. Always agree to a price before you allow someone to take you on a trip. Never take your wallet out in front of strangers. Don't get into an unmarked car with a stranger you can't communicate with, and certainly don't let them take you to remote and unknown places in an unfamiliar country having abandoned your only means of transportation in a separate country altogether – all the while sitting next to the only other person on the planet who knows where you are. Walter and I were far more than tipsy on wanderlust: we were idiots.

Wanting to put this whole messy business behind me, I gave him all the Armenian *dram* I had. It equated to roughly $50 U.S., which goes a long way off the beaten path in Armenia. He snatched the cash and counted it before stuffing it into his glove box. He then turned back to us and repeated the motion for 'pay me'. I protested and explained I had given him all the Armenian currency I had. Of course, my tone and countenance were all he could really go on since he didn't speak English. Angry, he yelled and loomed closer to Walter and I in the back seat. I conceded and gave him a few Georgian *lari,* which he also snatched and stashed in the glove box. I couldn't afford to give him any more money; we needed the rest to get home. *Marshrutkas* are cheap, but they aren't free. He was still not appeased. He made an attempt to grab my wallet but I leaned back in time to save it from his grasp. He began to yell and grow ever more agitated.

We thought about getting out of the car to make a run for it. But I realized doing so would only lead to an even worse situation. We would be alone and abandoned atop an Armenian mountain, unbeknownst to anyone, with no way of getting back home. We needed the car to get out of this. Left with no other option, I began yelling as menacingly as I could at our driver, who had now earned the title of 'kidnapper' as far as I was concerned; he was indeed holding us against our will. It was a fairly mild kidnapping, all things considered (it took place entirely inside a car), but it was still rather unpleasant.

Our kidnapper may have had the logistical upper hand, but he was outnumbered. Walter and I yelled angrily and the kidnapper yelled back. This went on for an embarrassingly long time, as I recall. In fact, we were running out of threats and I didn't feel it was nearly as menacing to repeat the same phrase over and over. Of course, our kidnapper didn't speak English anyway. We couldn't understand his stream of verbal abuse any more than he could understand ours. That meant as long as our *tone* was menacing, it would suffice. I changed tact and began screaming random words as violently as I could: "Tugboats! Charts! Marzipan! Jelly donuts! I pledge allegiance to the flag!" and so on.

Walter thought I was losing my mind, but soon joined in: "Arctic foxes! Put your own mask on first before assisting other passengers!" As tense as the moment was, it became a fun game to scream random things angrily... Go ahead. Take a moment in a remote place (bring this book with you) and scream harmless words vehemently – it's cathartic!

At long last, and most likely because our kidnapper was getting hoarse and may well have run out of words to scream at us, he stopped. We stopped. We sat in uncomfortable silence. Eventually he muttered something under his breath and started the car, reversing away from the cliff (which meant having to look past us through the rear window – awkward). It was an unimaginably uncomfortable drive back down the mountain. Our kidnapper was angry; every now and then he'd raise his voice, to which Walter and I would immediately and passionately release a small warning shot of furious (though mundane) words, and he would quiet down again.

When we reached Alaverdi, Walter and I leaped out of the car at the first possible moment and ran for it. I'm pleased to say we did eventually make it back to Turkey (amazingly, our vehicle was waiting for us). And while I have to admit it definitely gave Walter and I a story to tell, I also acknowledge that my thirst for wanderlust put both my and one of my best friend's safety in jeopardy. I would have had a hard time forgiving myself if my recklessness had resulted in anything happening to him.

WANDERLUST AND RESTLESSNESS

Admittedly, I have long heard the seductive song of wanderlust, the call to venture on and not stay in one place. I'm pleased to say I'm far better now at not being an idiot about it. In some ways, I feel very lucky to have the magnetic pull of change tugging so enticingly. *'One of several reasons for feeling restless is being drawn to a sense of adventure which is brought about by a life lived exploring new places. TCKs know there is a big world out there to explore. That can be a positive reason for many – being willing to do things a bit outside of the box, which becomes a gift, a characteristic that is sought by companies in the 21st century.'*[1] It means I'm more inclined to try new things, to meet new people, and see new places (while employing common sense and not getting myself kidnapped, of course). For me, the constant desire to move or travel has been a continuation of my childhood. *'Many TCKs who have grown up in the international community will continue to live and work in this community or one with extensive international roots.'*[1] Moving and traveling is how I grew up, and I have chosen to situate my life so I can continue that trend. Personally, I'm glad I did so; I find it very satisfying. That's not to say it doesn't sometimes cause problems, however – even when I'm using common sense.

The wanderlust and restlessness can cause challenges when it comes to relationships. For instance, at the moment I live in Belgium, and I have some marvelous friends here. Land of waffles and chocolate, Brussels is a very international city, full of people who understand what it's like to exist amongst different cultures. As much as I enjoy my friends, I am painfully aware of a developing trend. Whenever someone suggests an upcoming event, party, or adventure, people get on board: plans are made, dates are set, calendars are marked. When I'm invited, it's always prefaced with, "Are you going to be around then? Well if you are it'd be great to see you, but if not, we understand." Everyone assumes I'm a 'maybe' (at best) for events because I'm gone so often.

Admittedly, this is my own doing. I am gone a lot, and people have noticed. *'Too often, TCKs do not have the time they need to develop lasting relationships that affirm them or stay rooted long enough to develop a sense of belonging. This is why they feel they belong everywhere and nowhere.'*[2] This is the downside of my wanderlust (such a great term, by the way: *wanderlust* – I find it's best pronounced in its original German accent). My frequent travels make it difficult to maintain any sort of normal social life. While it does mean I more often get the, "So good to see you! It's been so long!" fanfare, it also means I miss out on the familiarity and consistency that help in building tight-knit friendships. I have to work much harder at those.

Not everyone wants to continue the highly mobile or continually transitional lifestyle they grew up with. Plenty of TCKs, once given the ability to decide their own path, choose to live a more stable life. Even those who choose stability over transition often struggle with feelings of rootlessness or restlessness. I have a friend who firmly decided to embrace a life of consistency after moving around a lot as a child. She doesn't regret her decision, but admits she has to rearrange all the furniture in her house every couple of years to keep the routine call for change at bay.

Wherever your personality leads you on the sliding scale of anchored vs. impossible-to-nail-down, it's important to strike a balance that's uniquely right for you. My lifestyle isn't for everyone, but it is for me. Many people would be horrified at the thought of being on the road (or in the air) as much as I am. But it energizes me. The compromise is that I must make concessions others wouldn't when it comes to maintaining deep and consistent relationships (which everyone needs in order to be healthy). I take more initiative to stay in touch and I arrange my schedule to prioritize time with people. Those who choose to spend time in one place may need to budget for travel more than their neighbors. If staying in one place makes you happy, but you still get the itch to see the world, it simply means you'll have to make concessions to do so. As a fellow TCK put it, *'When you are so used to leaving you grow restless being in a place too long. I feel like I will be able to put that feeling at bay by continuing to travel once or twice a year to a new place. Because that's all it really is; a strong feeling to see more, because you know more is out there that is beautiful and different than any other place you've seen.'*[3]

One of my very good friends says that for him, saving his money to take at least two international trips each year is more important than buying a bigger TV or a nicer car. To his friends and neighbors, for whom travel is not as high a priority, this doesn't make a lot of sense, but their desires are different. We all need community and a place to belong, but many of us, as

TCKs, also need mobility. I don't believe one must be sacrificed for the other – balancing both can mean finding arrangements that seem unorthodox to non-TCKs, but it's worth it. The career you pursue, how you budget your time and money, as well as how you prioritize your needs are all part of a customizable mix that varies based on personality and upbringing. You've got to build a mix that makes you feel at home. 'Home' can be a difficult word to define for TCKs, and perhaps the meaning will continue to change over time, and that's okay. *'Home is somewhere between here and everywhere.'*[4]

LIVING IN THE NOW

Regardless of whether the wanderlust or the 'stabilitylust' (I think there should be some sort of term to mean the opposite of wanderlust that sounds just as catchy) is strong in you, another characteristic that often accompanies the TCK lifestyle is an appreciation of *now*. I remember flying out of London's Heathrow airport some years ago and waking up on the bus just outside the terminal in time to see a giant billboard advertising a mobile phone network. It boldly stated, 'Everywhere in the world, it's the same time: NOW.' I thought this was genius. Time zones may have been around for a while and they may wreak havoc on my sleep patterns, but they're still an amazing and useful construct. Despite these manmade measurements of time and systems ensuring that even with the earth's rotation we all get to work or play in daylight and sleep at night, the truth is that *now* is constant everywhere.

Live in the Now, but Don't Get Kidnapped

It may sound obvious to be aware of the *now* but it's surprisingly easy to take for granted. Far too often, people don't appreciate the now because they're hoping for something in the future. Or they're not focused on the now because they're longing for things past. To truly live in the present is a discipline. For TCKs, the knowledge that you will almost certainly leave where you are now for somewhere new, and the realization that the set of circumstances you are part of at the moment are temporary can bring a heightened appreciated for the value of 'now'. Because of frequent transition in many aspects of life (leaving people or them leaving you, a new place to call home, a new culture to be immersed in), you may see more clearly that you've got to enjoy what you have while you have it. Nothing lasts forever. This may be harder to appreciate for people who experience change and transition much more slowly.

As a result, TCKs may more frequently take opportunities while they can, are often more inclined to seize the moment, and commonly value *now* as something to be enjoyed – something that can't be saved or stored, but can be wasted.[5] As with so many things, however, there are potential challenges if living in the now goes too far. Focusing *only* on the now can lead to making impulsive decisions. It can also lead to great annoyance for those around you if you live so much in the now that you don't bother planning for the future – even the not too distant future. People like to make plans, and can only include you in those plans if you commit to things in the future. Thus, overindulgence in now can lead to fear of commitment: if it doesn't pay off now, it's not on your radar. And while now shouldn't be wasted, there's a lot in life worth investing in and waiting for, as well.

Once again, balance is the key. In my experience, we tend to go overboard as a reaction to pain. For TCKs the pain experienced from frequent losses can drive us to embrace the now at the expense of anything else (even our own safety or that of our traveling companion). Perhaps we didn't realize how great a place was until after we'd left: we won't let that happen again, we'll enjoy every drop of where we are now. Perhaps we hurt from missing friends we've left or who have left us: we'll focus as much as we can on the people around us now. It really is a great skill to appreciate the now and live in it. But each now will become the past, and we learn from the past. Each now is birthed by the future, and we can plan for the future so that when it becomes now, we will get the most from it.

My friends, we *should* live in the now – it is a precious commodity and should not be wasted. But it should be balanced with an appreciation for the future and a respect for the past. Learn from those who've gone before you, and make plans to blaze great trails. That's how you'll make the most of now, collecting great stories to tell without running the risk of getting kidnapped.

If you like lists, this part's for you:

* Because of travel, exploration, and adaptation while growing up, many TCKs feel restlessness and even a migratory instinct well into adulthood.

* *'Many TCKs who have grown up in the international community will continue to live and work in this community or one with extensive international roots.'*[1]

* The restlessness and wanderlust TCKs can experience can also mean they find it harder to develop lasting relationships.

* Not all TCKs choose to continue in an international or transient lifestyle. Whether you do or not, you need to be comfortable adapting your life to the balance that's right for you. For instance, save money to travel if you stay based in one place, or pursue a career that allows for travel if that suits you.

* The transience TCKs experience can lead them to value 'now' very strongly because they know each experience is fleeting. Living in the now is good, but a balanced perspective that includes learning from the past and planning for the future will ensure each now is at its best.

---

[1] *Belonging Everywhere & Nowhere: Insights into Counseling the Globally Mobile.* Lois J. Bushong, M.S. Mango Tree Intercultural Services. 2013.

[2] *The Global Nomad's Guide to University Transition.* Tina Quick. Summertime. 2010.

[3] *The Worlds Within – An anthology of TCK art and writing: young, global and between cultures.* Summertime. 2014.

[4] *B At Home, Emma Moves Again*. Valérie Besanceney. Summertime. 2014.

[5] *Third Culture Kids, The Experience of Growing Up Among Worlds*. David C. Pollock and Ruth E. Van Reken. Nicholas Brealey America; Revised Edition. 2009.

CHAPTER 6

GOOD GRIEF, LOOK AT MY BRITISH TEETH

DEALING WITH FAMILY, NATIONAL IDENTITY, AND GRIEF

I have a tattoo. I'm very fond of it, actually. It's not huge, but it's meaningful to me. Tattoos aren't for everyone, and I strongly believe that they should be well thought through. Getting one is not a very good spur-of-the-moment overindulge-in-the-now activity. Growing up, my parents had a rule that we, their offspring, could not do anything permanent to our bodies until we were 18. Looking back, I think that was pretty wise of them. I'm pleased to say neither of my sisters nor I ran out on our 18th birthday and harpooned everything we could on our bodies or tattooed vast swathes of flesh. The rule drove home the importance of respecting permanence.

When I was 25, I got my tattoo as a gift from a dear South African friend (more about her in the next chapter). In Europe, 25 is the very upper limit of the age at which you qualify for reduced fares on trains, etc. It's officially the end of youth, at least as far as public transport is concerned. But I think it's also fair to consider it as some degree of adulthood: you've racked up a quarter of a century and that just sounds impressive. Even though I had a quarter of a century under my belt, getting a tattoo made me feel as if I were 18 and marking my independence. The funny thing is I didn't call my parents and tell them immediately after I'd done it. I had clearly abided by their rules, I was well over the 18-year threshold required for such an undertaking, and yet I couldn't bring myself to tell them.

I told my sisters, even emailed pictures to them, but still felt sheepish about revealing my ink to my parents. My sister, Gunch, thought it was absurd that I felt nervous telling my parents. Meanwhile, my youngest sister, Meg, had gotten one herself and had no issues whatsoever showing my mom and dad. Gunch was threatening to break the silence and tell our parents on my behalf (Meg was working on what I should get inscribed on myself next). Somehow, I managed to convince Gunch that I would tell my parents I had a tattoo when she announced she was pregnant. She wasn't pregnant at the time, and she and her husband weren't even thinking of having children yet, so I thought I'd bought myself some time. I had – about three years as it turns out.

I remember when my sister called to give me the good news: she was, indeed, going to have a baby. I was ecstatic! It meant I got to be an uncle, and being an uncle is a GREAT job. It's all the fun bits of having a child – spoiling them, playing, winding them up and feeding them copious amounts of sugar – with none of the bad bits: changing soiled diapers, punishing bad behavior, or dealing with the crash after a sugar high. I was busy imagining the fun I would have when Gunch brought up our deal: it was time to reveal my tattoo to the parents. My reasoning for striking such a deal was if we gave my parents great news and shocking news at the same time, they'd be so excited about a baby they wouldn't care in the slightest that I'd gotten a tattoo.

Gunch and I called my parents and after very little chitchat, she gleefully announced that a new baby would soon join the family's ranks. My parents burst into an excited frenzy of congratulations and expressions of joy, during which I announced I had a tattoo. My plan worked perfectly. Mom and Dad could not possibly have cared less – they were now grandparents! This annoyed Gunch terribly. She stopped all the fanfare and repeated to my parents that I had a tattoo. They politely remarked, "Oh, how nice," and continued on with talk about the baby. A perfectly executed plan if I do say so myself. I think the reciprocal of this agreement means someday, when I become a father, Gunch has to get a tattoo, but the exact terms for that part of the bargain are still being worked out.

I really don't know why I was afraid to share the news of my tattoo with my parents. There's not a lot of logic behind my strange fear: my parents are not the type to react badly to such a thing. In my experience, though, logic doesn't always reign supreme when it comes to the relationship between parents and their children. If you decide to stroll through a bookstore or scroll through one online, you'll find countless books on parenting. Being a parent is not an easy thing (which is why I've opted for the more-fun less-stress position of uncle for the moment). But I think it's also fair to say that being a child/kid/youth/young adult isn't exactly a breeze either. I have not noticed near as many books on how to be a good son or daughter in comparison to how to be a good parent. I'm nowhere near qualified to offer such a book, but I am fortunate enough to have spent time alongside sons, daughters, and parents and witnessed the complex dance that is being a family. I've confidently observed being a TCK can add some unique footwork to that dance – for both the parent and the child.

Projection

One very common cause of disharmony in the family jig is projection: presuming other people share your own feelings, stresses, joys, or concerns. Just as you can project an image onto a blank wall, you can project your own thoughts and feelings onto someone else... though other people are never blank. Because you're assuming things onto them, you miss what they're actually conveying. Parents do it to their children, and children do it right back. Projection is a different process than trying to instill values and beliefs – that is an integral part of a parent's job. Projection is more of an inability to read what may be going on with someone and, as a result, trying to fill in blanks that aren't really blank to begin with.

I met a mother once who confided in me she was terrified she'd done a bad job of parenting. She was confident her children were going to grow up to be nothing short of social reprobates incapable of leading normal lives, simply because of their table manners. I don't mean this particular mother was worried her children had a lack of table manners. In fact, her fear arose from quite the opposite – they had too many. The family had moved frequently amongst different parts of the world, each of which had their own rules for etiquette while eating. Brits and Americans use their cutlery differently, some Asian cultures use chopsticks, and other parts of the world forgo cutlery altogether (they design their cuisine to include edible scoops). This frantic mother observed that before her children would even take a bite in public, they would first survey the room to see what style those around them were using, and then mimic it themselves. This seemed to be an altogether too complicated and stressful routine to their mother.

I did my best to reassure her that having a broad vocabulary of table manners was not, in my experience, indicative of a looming descent into madness. It was more an issue of projection. For the mother, who had grown up in one culture, having to switch her well-ingrained eating style as an adult was a relatively stressful accommodation. For her children, who had learned many styles of eating in their formative years, it wasn't stressful at all. To them it was normal. They were not abandoning one established system to relearn a new one in its place. Their established system *was* to observe and use a multitude of table manners. Their mother was projecting her own stresses onto her children. Conversely, it's entirely possible she was missing real stressors in their lives because they didn't register as stressors in hers.

As much as parents do it, so do children. Kids may not be stressed about finding enough friends – school is full of people their age to build relationships with. But it may not be so easy for their mothers or fathers. Adults need friends to keep from getting lonely too, and they don't necessarily have quite the same captive audience as their school-aged children do. It's a tough discipline to bear in mind that not everyone is stressed by what stresses you or energized by what energizes you. Remembering this (and even vocalizing it) can help avoid miscommunication. This can lead to greater depth of understanding and empathy between family members. And research shows that TCKs *'who talked about close family ties despite geographical moves or distance ranked the highest on the well-being scores.'*[1]

NATIONALITY

Not only are people stressed or energized by different things (even within the same family), they also assign value differently. Another parent once questioned me about issues of national identity. This is a difficult subject for some TCKs and CCKs. The rigid concept of national identity doesn't always blend well with a TCK or CCK's characteristics and their myriad of experiences. I advised this particular father to avoid making any kind of assumptions and to watch out for projection. A parent who has adopted the international lifestyle as an adult often sees their nationality as an anchor – a constant which holds fast even when everything around them is changing. This is not necessarily the case for their offspring, who are growing up and forming their identities in the midst of constant change.

Parents may push for their children to have a strong sense of national identity based on their own origins and the comfort it brings them. This potentially causes problems in multiple ways. Let's take American military brats, for example. Many of the friends I grew up with had the same experience I did – they were technically American even if they had never lived in the U.S. for any significant period of time. Many of those who grew up believing they were American felt a lot of confusion when they went to America and found they couldn't relate to the identity they had always held onto. Many friends shared with me that going to the

United States for college or a job was a terrible shock. Although they looked and sounded like everyone else, they had been shaped by entirely different values and traditions. They had been told they were Americans – and honestly believed they were – but began to question it once confronted with 'actual' Americans who saw the world quite differently. It can be a very painful thing to suddenly discover the label you've clung to for stability isn't accurate at all. What's left to define yourself then?

On the other hand, some TCKs rebel against the concept of a national identity altogether. They don't feel it's an accurate indicator of who they are, and may feel far more aligned with the beliefs and traditions of the country they live in rather than the one that issued their passport. Parents who try to instill a strong sense of national pride in their children could perceive this as a personal rejection of their own beliefs and heritage: *'Parents frequently presume that their children see the world as they and the generations before them have seen it because they share a common national passport, so they are rudely awakened when a child does not behave according to expected practices.'*[1] In reality, it's more likely a desire to avoid being labeled in a way that can't reflect the experiences that come with a diverse and global upbringing.

As such, the 4th of July is a very confusing day for me. The two most prevalent cultural influences on my life growing up were the United States and the United Kingdom. It means I commemoratively celebrate a declaration of independence from myself each summer. It's as if I have multiple personalities that, for one day each year, are given a free pass to fight it out in my head.

The funny thing is, I don't think anyone else really cares – either in the U.S. or the U.K. I have not once seen headlines in the news heralding mass protests in the U.K. marking the rebellious breakup that transpired across the Atlantic with the former colonies. Nor have I read of the U.S. heightening security for fear of a hostile takeover from the land of tea and crumpets. Every now and then, mostly out of curiosity, I do wonder what it would be like if Her Majesty woke up one morning and decided she'd like the U.S. back in the British fold. I know, first-hand, how persuasive a British accent can be in the U.S.; perhaps she *could* seal the deal. On the other hand, I'm not sure the U.K. would go along with an offer from the U.S. to become the 51st state.

Despite the fact that nobody else is really bothered by my divisions of loyalty, each year during the observation of the United States' declaration of independence, I am. I've found myself passionately defending the U.K. while I'm in the U.S. on the 4th of July: pointing out great British contributions to the world. I've reminded Americans that they are charmed by British accents, castles, and quirks. I've highlighted the absurdity of simultaneously poking fun at how bad British cuisine is while hiring more and more British chefs on U.S. cooking shows. The conversation usually ends with me demanding innocent American bystanders take a close look at my teeth to prove to them that British dentistry is not as draconian or substandard as they assume. Generally people back down when you loom ominously with your mouth gaping wide, bearing your teeth at them.

I've also leapt to the defense of the Americans as my British friends question the wisdom of the former colonies departure from the empire. I passionately point out that huge contributions in fields ranging from technology to entertainment have come out of that independent nation. The U.S. is, by far, the most generous nation in the world when it comes to financial contributions by individuals. These conversations usually end with me removing layers of clothing and baring flesh to prove not everyone in the U.S. gets shot: I've spent time in the U.S. and I'm bullet-free! Admittedly, trying to take off your clothes and fling yourself at other people for inspection is about as effective in halting conversation as bearing your teeth at them.

Many TCKs have the rich and enlightening experience of being exposed to, and living in, several nations as they grow up. I maintain this is an amazing blessing and often fosters a broad worldview that will prove to be invaluable in our ever-globalizing world. But at the same time, this type of upbringing can lead to confusions of loyalty. I'm fortunate in that the U.S. and U.K. are friendly with each other. I do know of fellow TCKs, however, who are torn between two (or more) far less amicable nations. I can only imagine the amount of strain this can cause.

For a long time national identity was seen as an easy system by which to classify people. There were always exceptions, of course, but for the most part it was accepted that Brits were polite, Americans bold, Germans efficient, Japanese hard-working, and so on. Obviously, certain elements of that remain true –

cultural heritage, customs, and traditions often divide along national lines – but people are very complicated creatures. With increased access to long distance communication, cross-cultural trade and cooperation, migration, and greater ease in travel, the concept of people ascribing to a clear-cut, easy-to-categorize national identity isn't as clear-cut anymore. I'm not saying I think our referencing national identity to describe people or celebrating national pride in varying degrees is going to go away anytime soon. Global sports alone are enough to keep it going, if you ask some. But I do think we'll soon to have to appreciate that even if the borders aren't going to vanish, they are going to continue to blur. TCKs, for whom a more blurred system of national identity often fits more comfortably, can certainly struggle with explaining themselves to people (even parents) who hold to more traditional, easy-to-define categories.

MOVING

Issues like these boil down to projection and, frequently, an inability to clearly articulate feelings and beliefs. We can't find the words to say what we really mean, and so the words we do come up with are misinterpreted. This can lead to anger, hurt feelings, and frustration. Ironically, the times when we usually need the most cohesion are the times these issues are most frequently drawn out.

Take a move, for example. Projections are on full-blast because moving has very different effects on both parents and children. In a move, parents are usually very forward-looking; they've initiated or at least agreed to the move. They have things to do, and a timeline has been set in motion. They're facing forward because there is much coming at them that must be dealt with.

Meanwhile their children may be facing the completely opposite direction. Kids don't generally have much say in a move. Families are, as my mother always used to say, "at best, benevolent dictatorships". The kids go along because they have to, and when they do, they're usually looking back at what they're losing. They have difficulty facing forward because what's coming is unknown. What is known are all the things they're leaving behind, often against their will.[2]

So, parents often project their forward-facing stresses, while children project their backward-facing stresses, and everyone feels like no one understands. Additionally, *'members of a family do not process transitions at the same speed.'*[1] This means just because you've moved on from missing your old life to being excited about your new one doesn't mean your siblings have... or vice versa. It's easy to lose patience and project if you don't realize that while you're running the same race, you're doing so at varying paces (and for the sake of an amusing visual, sometimes even facing different ways). While there are no surefire ways to make a move, adaptation to a new environment, or the more challenging parts of life as a TCK stress-free, making every effort to communicate goes a long way. In the convoluted dance that is being a family, we're far less likely to step on each other's toes if we can communicate which way we're moving and why.

Often everyone thinks they're communicating when, in actuality, they're just projecting. Parents who take the time to not only listen to what their children are feeling (even if it means asking or answering seemingly annoying questions), but to also explain what they, as parents, are feeling stand a much better chance of keeping their families in rhythm. Likewise, kids who take the time to explain what they feel and are bold enough to hear what their parents feel gain a far better understanding of what is actually happening. Ultimately, reacting to reality is much more useful than reacting to a (possibly misguided) interpretation of what's going on.

Grief

Looking back, I remember one family move that caused an unparalleled quantity of tears – mostly from me. Many of the details of the move are now forgotten, as I was only nine at the time, but I distinctly remember looking out the window of our hotel through a torrent of tears just after flying to our new home. All my sadness stemmed from one small, seemingly insignificant object – a glow-in-the-dark toy owl. I can't remember where or when I had received my luminescent friend, but he'd been with me for some time. At that age I was fascinated with things that glowed in the dark. Luckily for this toy owl, not only was he an impressive bird of prey, he possessed that endearing ability to glow. He quickly became one of my more prized possessions.

My owl usually perched by my bedside, and his enchanting nocturnal luminosity meant he was the last thing I would see before falling asleep. I'd make sure he soaked in plenty of light to charge his glowing powers before I finally succumbed to the darkness of bedtime. While my parents had been making the final arrangements to leave, I had taken my owl on a trip to the park. I was out playing and cavorting with my sisters and somehow I must have lost him. In all the excitement and activity of our departure, I didn't notice he was missing until we'd already arrived in our new home, thousands of kilometers away.

After a frantic search proved unsuccessful, I'd taken my mother's sage advice to "remember the last time you saw him." Only then did I realize the last time I saw him was in the park of a far-off country we no longer lived in. I was devastated. Looking back, I think I was far more devastated than I should have been over a small glow-in-the-dark owl. He wasn't particularly expensive, or rare, or given to me to commemorate any special occasion. Nothing about the owl itself warranted the sadness I clearly remember feeling so deeply.

In hindsight, I realize I had attached much more grief to my owl's loss than the plastic animal alone was worth. All the sadness I felt from leaving the existence I knew had been focused onto one little glow-in-the-dark owl. My owl had been a symbol of consistency in my life and when I lost him, I wasn't just grieving his loss. I was grieving the loss of my world as I knew it up to that point.[3] Obviously, my world didn't end – it just changed – but I wouldn't be able to see that for a while. At that point in the move, I was looking *back* to what I had lost. I had no idea how many new adventures were *ahead* of me. Nor did I know that far more exciting things than a glow-in-the-dark owl would catch my attention.

Everyone deals with grief and loss. It's universal to the human condition. For TCKs, however, the events that cause grief tend to happen more frequently and the recovery time between them can be fairly short.[3] As a result, TCKs very often suffer from holding onto unresolved grief. After enough moves (either your own or those around you), it can feel a bit self-indulgent to dwell on the loss and sadness that occurs from such change – especially if that process happens repeatedly. *'Everyone has some mobility and associated losses in their lives, but for TCKs, the repeated cycles of separation and loss poses one of the biggest challenges they face.'*[1]

A friend once told me to write down every phone number I'd ever had. It took a while and seemed a rather futile exercise to me (not to mention it took a bit of research, I had dumped a lot from my memory). Having finally compiled the list, my friend said each of those digit combinations represented a sense of loss that needed to be expressed. It sounded crazy to me. Initially, I couldn't associate any sort of emotional response to the page of numbers in my hands. Eventually though, I remembered specific moments linked to each number. I recalled the places I had been when I dialed each one, asking for rides, telling my parents where I was, calling to frantically ask my father to bring something I'd forgotten to school, giving that number to a new friend, writing that number on permission slips for trips. Each of those phone numbers did represent an anchor in the chapters of my life that had since been closed.

I'm not saying we all need to jot down the phone numbers in our lives, but I do think it's worth bearing in mind that if grief goes unexpressed it will stay bottled up and eventually burst out unexpectedly. *'Cycles of transition give rise to multiple losses that result in grief that can come out in other ways.*'[1] To the outside observer, my emotional breakdown over a tiny glow-in-the-dark owl could have been perceived as irrational. In reality, the loss of my toy was simply a gateway to the release of sadness generated by my loss of so much more.

LET IT OUT

Grief must be expressed. This means it must be let out – it cannot stay hidden inside. Like communication in general, the way we allow what is on the inside (thoughts, feelings, or grief) to come out into the open varies greatly, depending on our own personality and style. Some people are gifted with words, some can create evocative art or music – we all have a multitude of creative channels at our disposal, but we've got to use them. Doug Ota, a grown CCK says it well, *'I have learned that grief is looking for the same thing I am: a story that makes sense.'*[1] The feelings on the inside are going to creep out whether we like it or not. We may as well address our grief head-on and maintain some sort of control over how it comes out, rather than letting it catch us off-guard, embodied in a lost toy or an inexplicable meltdown at an inappropriate time. Tina Quick explains, *'We, as humans, need to grieve our losses. We can get stuck emotionally until we recognize our loss and grieve for it. Grief validates all the good in our lives. Grieving well means recognizing and naming the loss, mourning the loss, accepting the loss, coming to closure, and moving forward to the next developmental stage.'*[4]

Being able to exert some control over the ways we express our grief means healthy and less destructive avenues of dealing with the challenges of moving and transition are available to us. Talking about our feelings, what makes us sad or stressed or angry, is not something everyone looks forward to. Personally, I find it a bit exhausting. Being vulnerable enough to express your feelings also means going through the effort of finding someone reliable who will listen (a hearty task perhaps, but one that's definitely worth the effort). I have come to realize, though, that even those of us who think of ourselves as internal processors still need to externalize from time to time. There's something hardwired into us as human beings that prevents us from being completely self-sufficient: we need community. We need others, even if only to help us define who we are individually.

Talking things out isn't simply for the sake of letting others help us (although, that is useful sometimes). We are often perfectly capable of taking action ourselves, we just need the igniting power of expressing our thoughts to someone else first. It's as if our thoughts and feelings and stresses are jammed into our heads where they're jumbled into a confusing, and sometimes overwhelming, mess. Letting them out not only allows someone else to see what's happening inside of us, it allows *us* to see what's happening inside of us. For TCKs who deal with grief more often and with less recovery time, being brave enough to intentionally express what's going on inside is a truly healing endeavor. It also helps those around us know what's going on. This sounds obvious, but how often have I been hurt or upset by someone else for not understanding my mood or actions when I haven't even bothered to communicate them?

VALIDATE

Even when we accept that getting grief out is necessary, it can prove to be a struggle. Parents, teachers, adults, and friends don't always know how to deal with grief when it comes at them. I'm writing this and I, myself, am guilty of not always dealing with other people's grief well – let alone my own. One reason I think people find it difficult to help someone else express their grief is that we seem to have an inherent and well-intended desire to move people to a happier place. If someone comes to us with sadness or struggle, we usually try to move them on to happiness. After all, who likes to be sad? It just seems like cheering people up is the helpful thing to do. I don't disagree that we should come alongside people and help them move from sadness to happiness, but that journey should really start with recognition and validation of their sadness. In a way, it's the idea that you can get where you want to go more easily if you know where you're starting from.

For example, I have often heard people say how sad they are at having to leave friends behind after a move. I've expressed those very feelings myself on numerous occasions. Quite often, the response to such expressions of grief is something along the lines of, "Don't be sad, you'll make new friends."[3] While this might be true (and a hopeful, well-intentioned gesture to move us away from sadness to a more positive outlook) it automatically ignores and invalidates the original feelings of sadness. It doesn't so much address the sadness as try to cover it up with something else.

We must be able to get our sadness and feelings of loss out so we know they're real feelings that happen for good reasons (we're not crazy, just human). We need to feel as if our sadness has been heard, and *then* we can start to move on to what the future holds. *'Offering comfort is a key factor in any grieving process... Remember, comfort is not encouragement. It is being there with understanding and love, not trying to change or fix things.'*[5] If we skip the initial step and don't have the opportunity to get our grief out, trying to heap happiness or distraction on top isn't going to make it go away. We risk feeling as if the sadness is wrong and is somehow our fault. When that happens, it stays inside, then festers and creeps out through whatever cracks it can find. We end up much more likely to have an unsightly breakdown in a public place caused by a seemingly unrelated trigger. I've seen it happen. It's not pretty and can be very alarming to the general public.

Control

Unresolved grief doesn't just lead to public meltdowns – if we don't choose to take some control over letting out what's bottled inside, it's entirely possible we'll become super-controlling over something else in our lives.[3] I have seen many examples (either in myself, in friends, or in other TCKs I've met along the way) of compensating for a lack of control in one area of life by becoming over-controlling in another. This behavior often baffles parents because the effects can seem far removed from the actual cause.

For example, one student, after arriving at my high school, became known as the 'Goth Guy'. He limited his wardrobe to black, decided pale was the new tan, and, in stark contrast to the colors around him, basically took to walking around school looking like a character from an old *Dracula* film. Apparently his new look started when he arrived at our school. It wasn't as if there was a large existing crowd of extras from old black-and-white movies he was trying to fit in with. He started this trend by himself, and it never took off as much of a trend. Seeing pictures of him from his previous school revealed his shocking former self – a guy who was not at all afraid of wearing colors. He looked like a completely different person.

It turns out he'd moved at very short notice to our school. His family hadn't planned on the move, and it all happened very quickly. He wasn't given nearly enough time for goodbyes or for properly letting go of his old world before becoming part of a new one. It seemed possible that 'Goth Guy' only really became that because he was desperately trying to control some aspect of his life amidst feeling as if he had no control over other parts. If he couldn't control where he lived – and that could obviously change at a moment's notice – then he was going to control how he looked. He could feel he at least had control over *something*.

Whether it's the way we dress, how we arrange our furniture, what we eat, or even when we exercise – if we don't feel we have control over a basic tenant of life, like location or being close to our friends (situations TCKs often find themselves in), we often project our need for control onto something else altogether. This misplaced need for control can manifest through very dangerous obsessions such as eating disorders. If the consistency we've tried to establish as compensation is threatened, we can react very strongly indeed. This is often confusing to innocent bystanders who don't know the root of our iron grip on some aspect of life. An unforeseen appointment means we can't get to the gym when we normally would; no big deal, right? If we've heaped all our hopes and dreams for control and consistency (displaced from somewhere else in life) onto a rigid workout schedule, we *can* react like it's a big deal. It may make us look crazy to the untrained observer or the unknowing parent, but it has less to do with a need for strict scheduling and more to do with feeling like we need some control in life.

Family Ties

Everybody experiences grief. But because TCKs experience it more frequently than normal and usually with less recovery time, we have all the more reason to focus on intentionally dealing with it rather than pushing it down and letting it fester. Going through the grieving process isn't something that can be done alone. This is all the more complicating since during a move, as one TCK put it, *'you're at a time in your life when you really need close people around you, and often, these people live on the other side of the world.'*[5] In light of this, don't forget that during a move the entire family experiences grief. *'Even though the family is moving from one place to another together, they are each experiencing the transition very differently. The move in itself has a separate meaning for each of them and the consequences of the move are so individual. Yet they will also one day remember them together as part of their family history.'*[6] Family members may each go through grief differently, but learning to face it and help each other through it will help everyone come through with more stability. *'Every family will have its own process for dealing with change, but repeated studies and anecdotal evidence indicates that if a family works together to keep open lines of communication and, while acknowledging their own frustrations and challenges during this period, parents manage to stay generally upbeat, usually children will do the same.'*[4] Within a family, everyone affects each other. Being willing to confront your own grief and struggles in a transition may help the rest of your family do the same.

IF YOU LIKE LISTS, THIS PART'S FOR YOU:

* Don't get a tattoo on the spur of the moment.

* Be aware of projection: presuming other people share your own feelings, stresses, joys, and concerns. People will project onto you, and you'll do it to them. It hinders us being able to really hear each other especially during emotionally draining times like a move.

* Be aware of issues involving nationality. It's worth remembering that your view may be far more fluid or blurred than that of your parents or other people who see labels like nationality as concrete anchors of stability.

* During a move, different family members have different perspectives. Times of transition can require extra effort in communicating to try and minimize additional stress.

* Everyone experiences grief, but TCKs usually experience loss that leads to grief more frequently and with less recovery time.

* Grief has to be expressed or it festers and can come out without warning at unexpected and inconvenient times. It's a much better idea to face it head on and have some control over how it's dealt with.

* *'Grieving means recognizing and naming the loss, mourning the loss, accepting the loss, coming to closure, and moving forward to the next developmental stage.'*[1]

* Don't forget to validate losses before trying to move on. We need to feel like our sadness has been heard, and *then* we can start to move on to what the future holds.

* Unresolved grief can cause us to become very controlling in some areas of life in order to compensate for feeling out of control in other areas that caused us loss and grief.

* Family members may each go through grief differently, but learning to face it and help each other through it will help everyone come through with more stability.

---

[1] *Belonging Everywhere & Nowhere: Insights into Counseling the Globally Mobile.* Lois J. Bushong, M.S. Mango Tree Intercultural Services. 2013.

[2] *What expatriate children never tell their parents.* Ellen van Bochaute. http://www.leuvion.com/public/uploads/13106297148700/ExpatKidsEN.pdf

[3] *Third Culture Kids, The Experience of Growing Up Among Worlds.* David C. Pollock and Ruth E. Van Reken. Nicholas Brealey America; Revised Edition. 2009.

[4] *The Global Nomad's Guide to University Transition.* Tina Quick. Summertime. 2010.

[5] *Expat Teens Talk.* Dr. Lisa Pittman and Diana Smit. Summertime. 2012.

[6] *B At Home, Emma Moves Again.* Valérie Besanceney. Summertime. 2014.

CHAPTER 7

BUDGET AIRLINES AND INTERNET CAFÉS

DEALING WITH ARROGANCE AND
BUILDING COMMUNITY

There is a certain budget airline in Europe (who, for legal reasons, shall remain nameless) that is singlehandedly responsible for causing unfathomable amounts of pain and suffering in my life. I daresay I am not alone. This airline flies passengers around Europe for unbelievably cheap fares – as long as you adhere to their strict, no-frills rules. And you don't mind being treated as slightly less valuable than livestock. And you don't mind landing at airports that are hours away from where they claim to be.

This particular airline seems to have been designed with the intent of making passengers deeply regret ever having considered flying with them. The misery begins online. Unsuspecting travelers are lured into the booking process with preposterously cheap fares, then trapped in a queue of never-ending web pages plying the tiny add-ons one must purchase to cover their basic needs. An extra €20 if you'd like to use the stairs to get into the aircraft; an extra €10 if you'd like to use the air vent above your seat; €5 per article of clothing you're intending to wear onboard the flight. While frugal, I doubt flying naked is nearly as fun as it may initially sound – how often do you think they *clean* the seats that cushion your bare bum and the bums of those before you? Your boarding pass MUST be printed before arriving at the airport. If you forget and wish to have it printed there, you'll pay a €70 fee. One can only assume the tickets are inscribed on gold filigree leaves using lasers shot from satellites orbiting earth – for security reasons, of course.

Once at the airport, the real fun begins. This airline intentionally sells 220 tickets for an aircraft that can hold 189 passengers. Budget airports purposefully

Budget Airlines and Internet Cafés

build terminals that go on for kilometers and have more gates than will ever be needed. This is done so said budget airline can whittle down its passenger numbers. There is no assigned seating, so travelers must queue at the gate in order to get a good seat. By queue, I actually mean fight to the death. A few excess passengers are usually lost in the process, but just to make sure, the airline will announce a gate change: "Evil Airlines flight 42653.3 from Obscure Greek Airport to Misleadingly Named French Airport announces a gate change. This flight will no longer be departing from gate 4; immediate boarding is now beginning at gate 426." It can be assumed that several passengers will lose their lives in the resulting stampede. Gate changes continue until only 189 passengers remain, thus profitably filling every seat in the cramped plane.

Onboard the fateful flight, passengers are bombarded with an overwhelming array of audio adverts at a volume so painfully loud they ensure any hoped-for rest is made impossible. Many passengers are eventually driven to purchase an exorbitantly priced inflight snack or drink to distract themselves from the ear-splitting torment, though to do so often requires taking out a second mortgage or swearing away one's eventual firstborn child in payment. The experience is not far from psychological torture; most passengers land exhibiting signs of post-traumatic stress. If, by chance, you survived the flight mentally unscathed, the journey from the airport to the city is sure to reduce you to tears. Often, the only way from the remote budget airport you've landed in to the city you're trying to reach is on the airline's own bus service, which will cost four times as much as the flight.

UNFAIR ASSUMPTIONS

It is a truly painful experience, but it does make getting around Europe relatively inexpensive. For me, the ability to travel cheaply led to *more* pain later on in life – it made me unrelatable to non-TCKs I tried to befriend. In the process of making friends, joint interest helps create bonds, and an easy way to get the process going is to share stories and experiences. While in the U.S. I heard a group of potential friends talk about their recent snowboarding escapades. I piped up and began to share my own comparable stories of snowboarding in Austria. Their reception to my tale was not what I expected. Rather than see what we had in common, my potential new friends saw me as different, spoiled, and clearly trying to one-up them.

It took me some time to realize that this was because travel is seen differently in the United States. It's a big country and it's considerably more expensive to travel internationally from than Europe. I was able to go snowboarding in Austria because I had flown the aforementioned evil budget airline to get there. I stayed in a hostel. The reality of my experience was far *less* glamorous (and significantly less expensive) than they assumed. I soon learned that while my international travels made me interesting initially, they were often a stumbling block to establishing real connections with people. As a result, I began to edit out location information from my stories in order to fit in better.[1]

A good friend of mine shared a similar experience when she arrived in Europe after living in South America. For her, travel wasn't the issue – housemaids were. Her father had worked for an international company in a particular South American country at a time when there was a definite degree of political unrest. As a result, her family was confined to a compound; they could not freely come and go without strict security measures being imposed. The company that employed her father also hired a housemaid for each family living on the compound. As a result, my friend grew up with a housemaid who was an active part of her family life. She had the same problem I did when she tried to relate to would-be friends in her new European surroundings. As soon as anyone heard her tell a story involving her family's housemaid (and many of her stories did, as while confined to the compound she spent most of her time with the people in her house), they assumed her to be showing off, rich, stuck-up, and different from them. They didn't understand that while having full-time house help is a significant expense in Europe, it was a non-optional, standard aspect of her life on the compound in South America. She wasn't trying to show off, it's just that her housemaid had been a big part of her life there.

Whether it's travel, housemaids, linguistic skills, dining etiquette, or any of the other countless factors that may come standard to many TCK upbringings, we often risk being seen as elitist or arrogant by our more traditional mono-cultural counterparts. The truth is TCKs can find it challenging to connect with non-TCKs. *'Remember that it is not you but your experiences that make it difficult for others to relate to you and you to others.'*[1] My youngest sister, Meg, moved from an international school in the U.K. to a local school in the

U.S. her junior year of high school. In doing so, she faced a far more difficult challenge than either my other sister, Gunch, or I had ever faced in dealing with transition while in school. Meg dealt with being *the* new kid trying to break into well-established and longstanding social structures. In comparison, moves between international settings are usually cushioned (at least a little) by the fact you're not the only one in transition; usually in those types of settings people moving in and out is normal. You're not alone as the new kid, you're part of the group of new kids. Accordingly, because social groups are always changing, they're easier to break into.

'Expat [international] environments make you so used to being in a diverse community. Moving into monocultural environments is deceiving because you might actually be 'different' for the first time in your life.'[2] Befriending non-TCKs or fitting into a monocultural setting is not an impossible venture, but it can take a bit of work. *'You don't need to hide or forget parts of your life, but it may take time for others to be ready to hear about them.'*[2] One obstacle to overcome in the process is to realize that the misperception is often reciprocal – not only do non-TCKs frequently have an incorrect view of TCKs, our perception of non-TCKs may be just as skewed. *'Be careful about assuming that the peers around you cannot relate to you just because they have never been expats. Give them the benefit of the doubt.'*[2]

More unfair assumptions

I recall speaking with a technical support engineer (based in the U.S.) on the phone while I was in the

Middle East. During the course of our conversation, the engineer asked why I was trying to fix my computer so early in the morning. I explained that where I was it was actually late evening. The concept blew his mind. He got terribly distracted (which is not what you want from someone trying to help you solve an annoying computer problem) by the idea that while he saw bright sunlight out his window, he was speaking to someone whose sun had set. He was not an idiot – he knew about the concept of time zones – but he was fixated on the idea that at the same moment, we were seeing two very different times of day out of our respective windows. I had known of and experienced this phenomenon since I was a child; I couldn't help but think my technician friend was a bit dim by being so fascinated with such a mundane situation.

Similarly, I had friends in the U.K. who marveled at the fact I carried around several currencies in my wallet and could keep track of the value of each in relation to the others. Again, this was something I had grown up doing. It didn't seem overly complicated or exciting to me, but to them it was an exotic and sophisticated way to live. Their fascination made me feel a bit superior – I *was* more worldly than they. And that's the problem. While TCKs may have to deal with non-TCKs perceiving them as being arrogant and elitist, the painful truth is that sometimes we actually are.[3]

Growing up internationally or in transition is not necessarily better than any other way of growing up. It's just different. It provides access to certain opportunities, and means there's a greater chance of picking up some skills as well as having to tackle some challenges.

But all varieties of the growing-up experience have their own customized set of opportunities, skills, and challenges. Don't get me wrong, I think (speaking as a TCK myself) we're marvelous. But others should think (and I hope they do) that the way they've been raised is marvelous, as well. What makes the world function in the fantastically diverse way it does is that different people groups, personalities, cultures, and traditions are exactly that – different.

As TCKs, the experience of growing up *between* cultures is hard to define and, therefore, sometimes overlooked. It would be a sad irony if by learning to appreciate our own *'culture of mixed cultures'* we failed to appreciate the uniqueness of others. In doing so, we would be causing the very problem we're seeking to resolve.

Listening to the stories and collective history of a group I befriended in the U.S., I came to appreciate that while they might not have the international travel savvy I did, they had an understanding of longevity and friendship I would have to work hard to attain. This group had known one another since they were small children. They had gone through varying stages of life together and still maintained consistency. They'd experienced puberty, a multitude of fashion trends, fights and heartaches, good times and celebrations, all together. While I benefited from being able to 'start fresh' each time I moved (and I certainly had a great collection of friends), I did not know the feelings of intimacy that come with knowing someone through so many stages of life and remaining an integral part of their story even to the present. There was a lot I could learn from them.[2] A good friend of mine (and fellow TCK) explained she always thought of her life as being a series of snapshots, while people with more continuity live lives that are a video. Non-TCKs are not inferior; they're just different. TCKs are not superior; we're just different.

The unknown is different for each person

When a friend of mine repeatedly talked (for almost a year) about how she was struggling with the decision of whether or not to move to Germany from the U.S., I eventually lost my temper. "Just move, for goodness' sake!" I finally erupted. "It's Germany, it's not Mars – you can make it work. You'll pick up the language, and if you really hate it, you can always move somewhere else. Quit waffling on about it and just do it. It's not that big a deal!" It was not, I should point out, my most shining display of compassion.

From my perspective, I couldn't understand how anyone could be so reluctant or stressed about moving. People move, it happens. It's not always easy, but we survive. I only realized my narrow-mindedness when someone asked me how I would react if I was given an amazing opportunity, but to take it, had to agree to live in one place for 10 years. That would have to be a pretty unbelievable offer. The thought of being restricted to one place for 10 years sounded like voluntary imprisonment. For me, constant change *was* normal. To step out of it into stability would result in a change so big it would definitely stress me out. For someone who has consistency as their normal, introducing change is stressful. We're two sides of the same coin; it's hard to move outside of what you're used to, no matter who you are. As TCKs, we should try to show the same open-mindedness to others that we hope to get from them.

Connecting makes the unfamiliar familiar

Open-mindedness is important in society today, especially as we continue to operate in a world that is more and more connected. Thankfully, connection is something TCKs tend to have a knack for. Sprinkling an awareness for the need to *not* be arrogant or elitist on top of that instinct means we've got a lot to offer in the world. I've seen TCKs in action and witnessed first-hand the impact they can have.

Let's take my dear South African friend, for example. The first time I ever met her she barged into my living room unannounced and made herself at home. It was during a time I lived in the U.K. at a place affectionately dubbed 'the Faulty Flats'. This was an aging manor home with the cheapest rent around, so it was the obvious housing choice for a young adult such as myself. I was working at a nearby U.S. military base, and not only was the Faulty Flats affordable, it was conveniently located just outside the base.

In exchange for its excellent location and attractive price, the Faulty Flats did have a lot of, shall I say, 'character'. The once-magnificent house had been split into 10 apartments, a process which created various fun oddities around the building. There were stairways that led nowhere, doors that opened to a wall, walled-in passages no longer connected to anything, and a fantastic basement (dungeon in our minds) complete with hundreds of years of discarded junk. The walls were pitted with holes and pocks, the floors slanted at odd angles, and the windows were as frail and temperamental as human beings tend to become at the same age. It was a strongly enforced rule that you could not sneeze in close proximity to any of the larger windows, as the quick change in pressure caused by such a blast from someone's face was enough to crack the ancient glass panes.

My part of the Flats comprised of a ballroom with fantastically high ceilings and large (but fragile) bay windows looking out back into what was once the garden, but had since been paved to become a parking lot. I also had a kitchen, bedroom, and bathroom that were originally servants' quarters, and were all very snug in comparison to the large ballroom. It was an odd combination, but it worked for me. To compensate for the 'less-than-new' appearance of the pitted walls, I covered every square centimeter I could with flags, posters, odd collections, and airplane 'barf bags' – whatever I could find to add color and detract from the derelict style that pervaded my part of the building.

Being that I worked on a military base, most of my friends were military. The majority of them lived in dormitories, and many found the open space of my ballroom, and the freedom afforded by the Flats, to be a welcome break from life in the dorms. So, many of my friends were around a lot. By 'around a lot' I mean several of them just moved in. Because of the variety of schedules held by everyone in their various military career fields, there wasn't a time the Flats didn't have someone in it. As a result, we never locked the door – people came and went at all hours of the day or night. It was generally a jolly place and could easily have one or two dozen people watching movies, eating food, or causing general mayhem at any given time.

One particular Sunday afternoon, a collection of my chums and I were relaxing in the ballroom. Some of us were watching a movie, many were multi-tasking by glancing between a laptop screen and the TV screen, and most were enjoying a cup of tea. Tea was definitely the official drink of the Flats. As most of my friends were American at the time, I took it upon myself to introduce them to the concept of a 'good British cuppa' with milk and sugar. The result was that we easily blew through 30 or more cups of tea each day. Most of the cupboards in the kitchen contained mugs – not food, not cooking implements, not ingredients – just mugs.

As we sat enjoying our tea, conversation, and various forms of media, a girl walked through the front door. She took a quick look around and then asked in a refreshing South African accent how she could get on the Internet and could she have a cup of coffee? I had never seen this girl before in my life, but assumed by her apparent familiarity she must be a friend of someone else in the room. In an attempt to be accommodating, I directed her to a vacant laptop and went to the kitchen to try and figure out how to make coffee (I'm not kidding – it really was a tea kind of place).

The other guys in the room all assumed I knew her, so they accepted the new guest and carried on as normal. I found some instant coffee and returned to the coziness of the ballroom with a cup of the stuff. I thought it odd no one was engaging this unique (and female – we didn't always get many of them) addition to the room. Whose friend was she? Apparently, the guys were thinking the same thing, assuming she was my friend and wondering why I wasn't catching up with her. We all sat in quiet wonder, not knowing what to do for some time. Finally (after about 20 minutes of secret pondering on the part of the boys in the room), the girl stood up, handed me the laptop, and asked how much she owed. I wasn't entirely sure how to respond.

"I beg your pardon?" I answered. She repeated the question and pulled out her purse, ready to pay. "Where do you think you are?" I asked in the honest sense of the question with no intended sarcasm. In an exasperated tone she explained she was friends with someone next door (another of my airmen buddies) and that his Internet was out. He was busy with some sort of project and told her to go around this side of the building where she could find a place to use the Internet and get a drink. She assumed after walking through the wide open door into an over-the-top decorated room full of people on laptops (I didn't think it was over-the-top) that this must be an Internet café.

The room burst into laughter. I tried to contain myself, not wanting to make her feel embarrassed. I managed to pull myself together enough to explain this was not, in fact, an Internet café; this was my living room. She turned bright red, let out a string of apologies, and hurriedly fled the room. It was so surreal that those of us who remained talked about it until we were interrupted by the return of our South African guest, about 15 minutes later. She walked in, apologized again, and then asked us to explain what exactly we were all doing there. How did so many people live in one place, why was the door wide open, and why didn't anyone stop her from barging in – in fact, why would we offer a stranger a *laptop* and a *bad* cup of coffee? (I really don't know how to make coffee).

We spent a fantastic evening trying to explain the Flats and how we were all connected by the nearby military base. Colleen was fascinated and stayed. I don't mean she moved in, but she became a very regular guest in the house and took part in all sorts of adventures that made up the legendary chapter of our history in the Faulty Flats. (She even paid for my tattoo as a birthday present a few years later.) She also got a job as a manager at a nearby restaurant. This was great news for us: leftovers were a rare prize in a house filled with domestically challenged men. What I really appreciate about Colleen, though, is that she bravely moved into a community completely alien to her in many cultural ways, latching on to the shared need for company and actively contributing to it. Colleen is one of the most open-minded, easy-to-connect-with people I know, and I've learned a lot from her. In many ways she embodies a skill TCKs use out of necessity – the ability to become a part of various groups and build the necessary bonds and links to make it work.

Community is worth some creativity

Sometimes making it work requires thinking outside the box, and that's the beauty of necessity – it can push you to creativity. The Flats taught me a lot in this respect. The benefits we receive from community and real relationships are worth the investment of some inventive thinking. One of the dynamics of a military community is people frequently get deployed. They're sent away for months at a time, often to remote places. Though they're gone, lots of things still have to happen at home. Bills must be paid, mail must be collected, houses or flats must be looked after, cars must be taken care of. Though it wasn't originally intentional, the Flats ended up being a tremendous help to single people dealing with deployments. An entire fleet of vehicles, representing all the people deployed at the time, was often parked in my back garden. We could use the cars as needed. There was no reason for me to own my own vehicle – I could choose from a selection of those left in my care. A giant folder was compiled containing everyone's powers-of-attorney to take care of financial matters in their absence. It became a regular occurrence for me to go to the bank and move thousands of dollars of other peoples' money around to pay their various bills. We would also take the folder to the post office and collect stacks of mail for everyone.

Christmas was a big deal at the Flats. For many people the need for community is felt all the more sharply at a time traditionally spent with family. To compensate, we'd go as far overboard as we could. The process of decorating for the holidays wasn't complete until it looked like Christmas itself had thrown up in glittery fervor all over the Flats. Christmas music took exclusive hold and was the only sort of music allowed to waft through the ballroom. We all committed ourselves to Christmas in a very big way. Looking back, I am continually amazed at how much everyone got into the spirit.

The holiday fervor was so great that we had to get liberal with the date of Christmas. Some of the regulars at the Flats happened to be deployed over December 25th and demanded they be able to celebrate a delayed Christmas when they returned. As a result, decorations would stay up for several months into the new year. Alternatively, there were those who would be flying back to the U.S. for the holidays, but still wanted to take part in a Faulty Flats Christmas. So, in order to accommodate a celebration of pre-Christmas, decorations went up even earlier than normal. It got to the point we were decorating for Christmas in early October and didn't un-decorate until March. Christmas was occupying half of the year – and we were okay with that. It became so normal to us that I distinctly remember being annoyed when I couldn't find any Christmas decorations for sale in September.

ENDANGERED COMMUNITY

Silly things like Christmas lasting half the year and the practical 'everyone-takes-care-of-everyone' aspect of the Faulty Flats made strong impressions on people. Quite frequently, after someone moved away from the Flats they would make regular phone calls back to chat with those they had left behind. I found this happened most often with people who returned 'home', or at least to their home countries, after being abroad and living at the Flats. Initially, I would gladly offer updates on the latest developments – what we'd managed to blow up in our experimental microwave (we had one microwave for cooking food, and one exclusively for exploding food products), who would next be moving in or out, etc. But after a few phone calls I always felt I should encourage them to focus on writing a new chapter in their lives. Previous tenants needed to take what they had learned from the Flats and build on it, figuring out how to include the people around them and increase community in their new homes.

I only realized later on in life what a difficult task I was asking people to undertake and how different it was from the transitions I was accustomed to. My moves had mostly been to other international locations – I had never repatriated or returned 'home' (to be fair, I'm not entirely sure where I would call home). My experience of moving on was entirely different to that of someone returning to a familiar environment, and I deeply regret not being more understanding to those who undertook this deceptively complicated endeavor.

One of the challenges people often faced (that I wasn't aware of at the time) was a weakened sense of interdependent community, compared to the one often found amongst displaced people in a foreign land. What we had at the Flats, and what many people who live in international communities take for granted, is a powerful blend of factors that are hard to recreate in more traditional environments. Often people find a strong sense of belonging among others who don't belong. Foreigners don't feel so foreign around other foreigners.[4] I feel people who have been fortunate enough to experience a true sense of belonging and community have an increased responsibility to share and recreate it for others. Community is not easy for people to find in the world these days, so we've got to help.

One particular night, I came home to the Faulty Flats very late. It was easily 2 a.m. and I was exhausted from having to work late on some big projects that were coming up. As I pulled into our parking lot, I was horrified to see there wasn't a single parking space left for me. I couldn't even park at my own home. Disgruntled, I drove down the street, parked, and complained to myself as I walked back to the house. I went inside and was immediately greeted by a young man I'd never met before. He was incredibly welcoming and ushered me through to the kitchen. He introduced himself as Aaron and proceeded to make me a (very welcome) cup of tea. He asked how my day was and shared a little about himself. Midway through our conversation he interrupted himself to ask if I was planning on staying the night.

I realized this man clearly had no idea who I was. He wouldn't have asked if I was planning on staying the night if he knew that it was, of course, my home. Without further explanation, I said I really had hoped to sleep over. He made a very apologetic face. Then he explained that because it was so late, most places to sleep around the Flats were already occupied, but he thought he could squeeze me in on one of the larger mattresses in the bedroom if I didn't mind the close quarters. I was well aware of the rule: first come, first served. So after a very pleasant chat with Aaron, I found some blankets and claimed my half of a mattress in the bedroom.

The next morning was Saturday and I awoke to the sound of cheery conversation and the smell of home cooking wafting in from the kitchen. Cooking was definitely a novelty in the Flats and worth waking up for.

I wandered into the kitchen to find Aaron cooking eggs, toast, and bacon. I'm not entirely sure where he'd found such things, but I was thrilled. The other regular guests at the Flats were gathered in the kitchen, clearly in awe of this culinary spectacle too. Several of them greeted me as I stumbled in. Aaron smiled and exclaimed how great it was I already knew some people there. At this point, one of my other friends pointed out it was only natural I should know the people staying in my own house (ironic since that clearly wasn't always the case). Aaron stopped what he was doing as embarrassment spread red across his face. He began to apologize, but I quickly stopped him (and not just because I wanted him to continue cooking). I explained how I felt truly honored to be welcomed so graciously in my own home. It meant a lot to me that people felt so at home they took it upon themselves to welcome others – it was living the dream!

That's the dream I think we've got to pass on. If we've experienced the close-knit camaraderie that often comes from living in a community abroad, we've taken part in something which is becoming less and less common around the world.[5] Technology and other advances mean we're able to live more and more independently and place a higher and higher value on privacy. I'm not saying we should go against those things, but I am saying if we don't have some sense of balance, we can easily trample over the healthy *interdependence* that binds people together.

IF YOU LIKE LISTS, THIS PART'S FOR YOU:

* Beware of budget airlines.

* So you don't come off as unapproachably exotic or as if you're trying to outdo someone, it may be helpful to edit out details like location when building relationships with non-TCKs.[1]

* Bear in mind you might be perceived as being more arrogant than you really are because of your travels and experiences; but also bear in mind you might be acting arrogantly if you assume non-TCKs are inferior. In truth, you have as much to learn from someone who's grown up in a stable environment, as they do from you.

* If you're comfortable in transition, don't assume everyone is. You might be as scared of stability as they are of transience.

* As a TCK or CCK, don't take your ability to make connections for granted. Having to adapt to new people and places builds up your interpersonal skills so you can meet your need for community even in seemingly unfamiliar places. Hone those skills because the frameworks community builds on are becoming more and more rare in the world.

---

[1] *The Global Nomad's Guide to University Transition*. Tina Quick. Summertime. 2010.

[2] *Expat Teens Talk*. Dr. Lisa Pittman and Diana Smit. Summertime. 2012.

[3] *Third Culture Kids, The Experience of Growing Up Among Worlds*. David C. Pollock and Ruth E. Van Reken. Nicholas Brealey America; Revised Edition. 2009.

[4] *The Art of Coming Home*. Craig Storti. Intercultural Press Inc. 1997

[5] *Bowling Alone: The Collapse and Revival of American Community*. Robert D. Putnam. Touchstone Books. 2001.

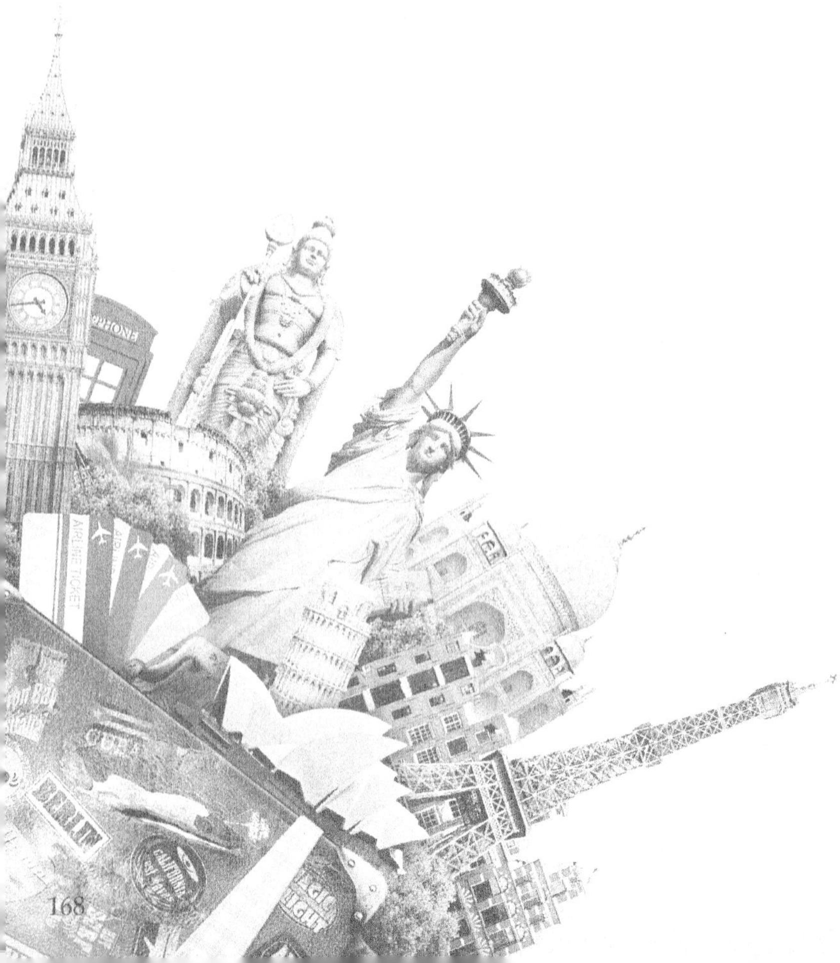
PHONE
AIRLINE TICKET

CHAPTER 8

GLOBAL TRENDS IN TRAIN LIBERATION

THE WORLD IS CATCHING UP TO THE TCK EXPERIENCE, SO WHAT DO WE DO?

Back in the days when the Faulty Flats was still in its infancy and not yet a hub of thriving community silliness, my sister, Gunch, lived in the apartment above me. As neighbors, we scraped out a pretty meager existence. We didn't make much money (our reason for moving to the Flats in the first place), and we conserved every way we could: carefully scheduling the days I would heat my apartment so Gunch could benefit from the heat rising into hers; switching on the lights only for the room we were actually in. We subsisted on baked beans and toast, which was surprisingly cheap. If you didn't mind eating nothing but beans on toast, you could do so for just £10 per week. It wasn't the healthiest of diet plans, but it was the most cost effective.

One expense we couldn't avoid was transportation. Gunch and I worked between two military bases in close proximity to us. While one was down the road and the other a 15-minute drive away, we still needed cars to carry us to and from our respective jobs. Unfortunately, our schedules did not mesh up well enough to share a vehicle – we needed two. Luckily, through the marvelous generosity of various friends unable to take their vehicles with them when they left the country, we actually had three cars between us.

Our small fleet consisted entirely of Volvos. In honor of their heritage, we felt it appropriate to give them all Scandinavian sounding names. There was Sven – a midnight blue, boxy Volvo 740 with an overly elongated front and an equally elongated rear. Sven had been our faithful family vehicle for many years and when my parents and youngest sister, Meg, moved away from the U.K., they left Sven in the able care of Gunch and I. Though Sven remained trusty and reliable, he had some quirks. First, there was the daily door lottery. Sven would seemingly at random decide which of his four doors would respond to the commands of the central locking system. The doors could not be manually unlocked, so you really were at the mercy of his temperament when it came to vehicle entry options. Sometimes only the front passenger's door worked, sometimes you were lucky enough for it to be the driver's door, sometimes only a rear passenger's door would work and you'd have to climb up to the driver's seat hoping no one was watching the odd, but unfortunately necessary, spectacle. Sven also had a hot temper. His cooling system was dodgy at best and so he'd overheat very easily.

Next was Olarf, the less boxy but still very angular Volvo 340. Olarf was silver and considerably smaller than Sven. He had a manual choke, which meant he enjoyed waking up and starting on a cold winter morning slightly less than I did. For the most part Olarf operated without complaint. In fact, his one real fault wasn't his fault at all – it was the result of Gunch and I overestimating his off-road capabilities. We'd taken him down a very uneven farm road a bit faster than we should have, and a particularly jagged piece of protruding ground dislodged his protective undercarriage. Gunch and I tried to reattach it with a creative combination of twine, duct tape, and bungee cord, but we eventually gave up and resigned ourselves to the fact Olarf would carry us through life without any underwear. By that I mean Olarf had no underwear; as a responsible driver, I did.

Finally, there was Thor. Thor was a mighty red Volvo 240 and will certainly outlive us all. Built like a tank, and almost certainly weighing as much, he could pummel his way through just about anything in his path (though, as a rule, we tried not to use him for ramming purposes). Thor's one peculiarity was that he was not a fan of cold weather. He would scream like a banshee if driven in anything less than balmy temperatures. His squealing didn't last for only a minute or two – by the time we would reach the guard post of the military base 15 minutes away, Thor's squealing would herald our arrival at truly painful volumes (much to the annoyance of the guards on duty).

One would think that armed with this small squadron of cars, navigating our way through our transportation requirements would be simple. But this was sadly not the case. Each car's unique quirks reacted with various weather conditions. I must point out, in case you aren't aware, that the U.K. enjoys a wide variance in its weather. Great changes in temperature and precipitation don't just come with each new season; such an array of changes can happen each day – sometimes each hour. A day can start out cold and wet, be sunny and dry for lunchtime, and snow in the evening. It's all part of the British adventure.

Sven couldn't be driven when it was warm outside: he'd overheat. Olarf couldn't be driven when it was wet outside: without his underwear, water would get up into the engine and he would stall. Thor couldn't be driven when it was cold: his screams would terrify the wits out of anyone within hearing distance. The fact that our mode of transportation was so closely tied to the weather turned Gunch and I into amateur meteorologists. The simple task of getting to work in the morning required a survey of approaching weather fronts, high and low pressure zones, and historical records of annual rainfall.

Even with our exhaustive planning efforts, we constantly ended up in trouble. I would take Olarf to work in the morning on a seemingly warm and dry summer's day only to have a rainstorm creep in by the time I was ready to leave. I'd call Gunch; she'd head out with Thor to retrieve me, and we'd have to coordinate a rescue plan to bring Olarf back home when the rain had stopped. During the course of a week we'd constantly have to abandon cars, retrieve cars, and rescue each other from failed attempts to properly predict the weather.

More puzzle pieces to play with

Not many people have to operate with such a strong link between weather and transportation. I mean obviously good drivers are aware of severe weather hazards, but most people have vehicles that can withstand a reasonable array of adverse conditions. I've discovered over the years that TCKs, in particular, must often learn to function by tying together more sources of information than might normally be expected. Some Westerners living in the Middle East must connect language skills with motor coordination: as a left-handed person, I have to remember that if I hear Arabic, I must put my left hand in my pocket so as not to use it as my dominant hand and offend someone. People living amongst multiple cultures often have to process a wider variety of beliefs, values, and opinions in order to form their own view of the world. It's like being able to paint your life with an almost overwhelming amount of available colors.

This is no longer a phenomenon restricted to just TCKs. As the world continues to globalize, and we become ever more closely-knit financially, logistically, and technologically, *everyone* is being exposed to more and more information, varying cultures, and alternate points of view. Some studies have suggested that we, as people, are having a hard time processing all of the information coming at us. One experiment found people working in finance make worse decisions when they have a large abundance of data: they get overwhelmed. More information doesn't automatically mean better decisions.[1] How we process information into useful knowledge is what's important.

This is one area where TCKs seem to benefit from an upbringing which has forced them to make sense of significant amounts of diverse information. Moving to a different country or culture forces one to take in new information and make it useful. For example, food in the grocery stores of Southeast Asia is rather different from food in the grocery stores of Western Europe. Moving from one part of the world to the other doesn't mean you stop eating, so you've got to make sense of it. It seems obvious, but learning to do that successfully can be applied to other areas beyond food. Management styles in the Middle East differ greatly from those in South America, but if someone is in charge of overseeing the manufacture of a product made of parts coming from each area, he or she must adapt in order to communicate appropriately with both. *'In an era when global vision is an imperative, when skills in intercultural communication, linguistic ability, mediation, diplomacy, and the management of diversity are critical, global nomads are better equipped in these areas by the age of eighteen than are many adults. Why? Because they have spent years developing these skills as strategies for social survival in times of transition.'*[2] These skills are more and more sought after worldwide. The world is aligning ever closer with the experiences of TCKs.

MORE INFORMATION TO DEAL WITH

Globally, there is so much data available it's changing the way we perceive information and knowledge. Take Wikipedia, for example. Loads of people use Wikipedia – it's an expansive warehouse of information, and it's free. I can get caught for hours on Wikipedia if I'm not careful: I'll look something up, and as I'm reading about it I'll come across a link to something else interesting... and then the cycle repeats. I may have started out by trying to learn more about tea production in Sri Lanka and somehow, 10 minutes later, I've discovered there is a protein in humans that is actually called 'Sonic hedgehog' – no kidding. Apparently it's very important for the organization of our brains.[3] That particular leap of abstraction took just five clicks.

The thing about Wikipedia is it represents a shift in how we view and value information. Wikipedia is built by volunteers, it runs on donations. It's a real-time self-moderated community. That means there's no guarantee the information you're reading is true or accurate. The system does work pretty well and the majority of the time, it seems you can trust the integrity of what's posted... but it is essentially mob rule information. We believe it's true simply because most people say it's true.

It seems mob rule is more and more widely accepted as a viable system – though not for everything. There are still some areas of life that require standards and authority. Imagine if bank accounts shifted to mob rule like Wikipedia. You could go into a bank to withdraw $50 (which you're sure you have in your account because you keep an excellent record of transactions), but the bank staff decide (based on consensus among themselves) you only have $5. I can't see many people signing up for Wikipedia-style banking.

I believe part of the reason we're moving to more Wikipedia-style authority (or lack thereof) in various aspects of life is because we have an immense amount of information, and we're short on authorities to manage it. In some ways it's wonderful to have access to loads of raw data; it means we get to interpret everything ourselves. But that can be a daunting process, and it's part of what makes repeatedly being uprooted and replanted such a challenge for some TCKs. They've got to continually reinterpret new information. To thrive in a new environment, TCKs must take in the new data around them, then make decisions, build friendships, and figure out systems based upon it. Thankfully, many find learning to reframe life based on new environments and cultures eventually leads to some degree of comfort. Many TCKs feel they've moved enough, reinterpreted their environment enough, and made sense of enough new kinds of information to feel comfortable just about anywhere. They begin to trust in their ability to adapt. Having to make sense of varying information is only one of the challenges a lot of TCKs have been dealing with for a while. More and more, *everyone* is beginning to deal with these challenges. The world is aligning ever closer with the experiences of TCKs.

More need for conflict resolution skills

Earlier I discussed conflict resolution skills. TCKs can struggle with conflict because in transience, they often learn to make relationships disposable in order to keep themselves from being hurt. If you know someone is going to leave (or if you're going to leave) you don't feel obligated to fix things with them if a fight erupts – they might be about to 'expire' anyway! Thanks to social media, this challenge is not something only TCKs face now; everyone is combating the urge to dispose of people or avoid conflict.

People are not really dating unless it's 'Facebook official'. A couple hasn't broken up until it's 'Facebook official'. We know we're really friends with someone when a Facebook friend request reinforces what's going on in real life. More and more we're merging real life with life online. One of the resulting effects is that we're now able to delete or dispose of people quickly, online, without any awkward face-to-face interaction. So even non-TCKs now face the temptation of not resolving conflict; anyone can dispose of someone by deleting them as a friend. Because if you're not Facebook friends, are you really friends? Now, conflict resolution skills need to intentionally be taught not only to TCKs, but to everyone. The world is aligning ever closer with the experiences of TCKs.

MORE RELATIONSHIPS TO DEAL WITH

Earlier, I also mentioned that TCKs can feel overwhelmed by the amount of relationships they have. Again, it sounds silly to suffer from having too many friends – but we only have so much time in a day and only so much emotional energy to invest in people. TCKs struggle because their transient lifestyle exposes them to numerous people as either they move or the people around them move. Now even non-TCKs are becoming overloaded with friends because social media has put millions of people easily within reach. As a result, studies are finding we're spreading ourselves thinner.[4] We have greater quantities of friendships, but the quality is suffering: we're enjoying less depth in our plethora of friendships. Increasingly, it's not only TCKs who have to try to find a way to manage their extensive list of friends. The world is aligning ever closer with the experiences of TCKs.

MORE NEED FOR COMMUNITY

Speaking of friendship, TCKs have often been forced to be socially adaptable. When you're the new kid, you've got to actively go out and make friends. On the flip side, TCKs are often more accepting of new people and open to building friendships because we know what it's like to be the new kid. Mainstream culture is facing an increased need for people to actually learn the process of how to *make* friends. Traditionally, if you didn't move around a lot, friendships usually formed because of where you lived, went to school, or worked. You were around certain people often enough and long enough that friendships naturally formed. Now, a higher and higher value is being placed on privacy, so people keep to themselves more; and the world itself is becoming more transient as people move more frequently: people are changing jobs more often. As a result, friendships don't occur quite so naturally. The friend-making social skills that TCKs are likely to pick up because of their transient lifestyle are actually now needed by others on a much broader scale. The world is aligning ever closer with the experiences of TCKs.

More Definitions

As technology, the economy, and globalization rapidly change the world we live in and the way we interact with each other, I think we're going to see a shift in the way people define themselves. Many TCKs have long dealt with trying to find an expression for aspects of their identity beyond traditional cultural or national categories – mostly because they often exist in between those classifications.

Thanks to migration and increased mobility on a global scale, more and more people are looking for ways to describe a sense of core identity beyond a stereotypical label of nationality. People are zooming in and out, adjusting their focus to try to get a clearer picture of who they are, what defines them, and how they relate to those around them. Nationality certainly plays a part in identity, but it's a component, not a definitive label. This is clearly a shift from the more traditional categorizations used by previous generations, and it's one that TCKs and CCKs have been wrestling with for some time. The world is aligning ever closer with the experiences of TCKs.

THE FUTURE IS ARRIVING

'Third Culture Kids are the prototype citizens of the future.'[5] Truly, *'The TCK story is about to become nearly everyone's story.'*[6] In many ways, the future is already here. But being a bit ahead of a trend can be lonely. It's one of the main reasons I think TCKs may struggle so much with identity and why the need for terms like 'TCK' can be so helpful. Without accurate vocabulary to relate to, we can all too often try to compare ourselves to others using terms that aren't so accurate, and end up feeling alone in our uniqueness.

Even the term 'TCK' can cause problems. The need for identity, the ability to express that identity, and the sense of belonging or uniqueness which comes with it can drive people to compete about things that don't require competition. I've seen TCKs argue about their degree of TCK-ness. How many passports they have, how many countries they've lived in, and how many schools they've attended can all be reduced to a point system to show what TCK elite-status they have. I've even seen TCKs cling to their identity so strongly as to alienate non-TCKs, looking down on them as inferior. That's neither helpful, nor accurate. Whatever degree of TCK I am, I'm glad for the term. The ability to name something gives us the power to explore it: words set thoughts free from our heads and allow them to come out through speech or writing (or other useful avenues) to be shared.

Get Onboard

So, my people, what does all of this mean? If the world is aligning ever closer to the experiences of TCKs and CCKs, what are we to do? I believe that's best summed up in the story of the Croatian train liberation. For this story, it is essential for you to know I am not built for hot weather. My Scottish ancestry passed down genetic traits that would ensure I survived the wet and cold of the highlands, not the oppressive heat of... well, anywhere not covered in clouds or chilled by rain. In spite of global warming though, I manage – thanks in part to the wonders of air conditioning and in part to my almost vampiric ability to avoid the sun. I choose instead the more temperate climes of evening for outdoor adventure.

Even my sharpened aptitude for avoiding the heat is not always enough to evade every high-temperature situation, however. It is in these rare, though intense, predicaments that my ratio of common-sense-to-crazy begins to dip more dangerously than usual toward the far reaches of the unhinged lunatic end of the scale. Being hot reduces me to a crazed sweaty mass of agitated annoyance, gushing both anger and perspiration as I attempt to lower my core temperature and regain civility. It's not pretty (and probably doesn't smell pleasant, either).

On a trip through Eastern Europe with my fearless travel companion, Walter, I found myself quickly approaching heat-induced critical mass at the cruel hands of the Croatian Railway Service. We were heading from Zagreb to Budapest on a daylong train ride in the height of summer. We left the uncomfortably muggy main station in Zagreb at high noon. As we boarded the train, we were pleasantly surprised to find the second-class facilities in good shape and with space enough for most parties to enjoy their own cabin (each train car consisted of several six-seat cabins bordering a corridor that ran the length of the train car). This pleasant surprise was quickly stifled by the realization that all of the windows had been bolted shut – no cabin or corridor window was exempt. The whole car was on air lockdown.

As the train had been sitting in the hot sun for some time prior to departure, the lack of airflow had created nothing less than an oven into which passengers were loaded. I tried to remain calm. The initial stages of heat-rage were beginning to boil within me. Surely an air conditioning system would switch on when the train started moving, and this was the reason the windows were bolted: to preserve the cool, anger-suppressing air that would emanate from the vents prominently placed around the cabin. In a matter of minutes, every square centimeter of fabric unfortunate enough to be in contact with my incredibly powerful sweat glands was saturated.

Finally, the train lurched into motion and was soon at cruising speed on its way to Hungary. Admittedly, *something* had begun to proceed forth from the air vents. It was not, however, fresh cool air. It was like someone's warm breath. It was irritating and invasive and increased the sticky vexation of the situation more than I thought possible. This was not going to be pretty. Walter and I frantically tried fiddling with controls, forcing window bolts, and whimpering pathetically. The heat lunacy was almost upon me – I would soon be forced to claw my way through the side of the train just to create an air vent. Before giving in to the impending mania, I dashed out of the cabin and made my way to the doorway guarding the connection between our train car and the one adjacent to us. I flung open the door and was relieved to discover the area connecting the train cars was uncovered. It allowed a sweet rush of air to sooth my sweltering body, temporarily holding my heat-madness at bay.

At this point, I was prepared to perch precariously between train cars for the entire eight-hour journey. Walter tried to convince me this was neither safe nor practical: two ideals that, alone, could not motivate me to leave. Not overheating was of a higher order, in my opinion, than being safe or practical. Walter emerged a few minutes later from the sweaty cabin of doom to coax me out of the breezy inter-car gangway again. This time he was armed with a real bargaining chip: from his keychain hung a bottle opener just the right size to release the window bolts. I hesitatingly returned to our cabin. A pleasant breeze was now flowing through the open window; our compartment was livable and quickly approaching comfortable. I thanked Walter profusely, and we sat down to enjoy our journey.

After a few minutes, my mind wandered to the plight of all the other passengers. They were trapped in mini-heat-box-compartments on the train, probably sweltering into the same madness that Walter and I had before our release. There was only one thing to do: I announced (probably with more gusto than even Walter was expecting) that I had to liberate the train.

Armed with Walter's ingenious bottle opener, I made my way from one end of the train to the other. I burst into compartments filled with lethargic, sweaty, barely-conscious victims of heat exhaustion and boldly announced I would rescue them. Cabin after cabin came to life as the quick twist of a bottle opener filled their rooms with fresh air. Passengers gasped for it, cheered, and exhaled appreciation. Several passengers even tried to hug me (a gesture I violently opposed as so much skin contact may have fused us together in such heat).

As each cabin along the corridor became livable again, more and more passengers joined the rescue party. By the time we reached the last compartment, a gaggle of excited liberators had formed. The final car held a Canadian traveler who had resorted to stripping down in order to combat the heat. We had reached him before his bare essentials were... bared. The whole party erupted with celebration as the last victim was allowed to cool down, despite the best efforts of the Croatian Railway.

Amidst the revelry, I slipped out and headed back to my cabin where Walter and I relaxed in the knowledge that the heat had not overcome us. A few minutes into my rest the entourage of co-liberators found us and the celebrations continued. Walter was slightly alarmed, unsure of what exactly I had done to incite riot this time. He was quickly brought up to speed and thanked for his ingenuity in freeing the oppressed. As we journeyed comfortably toward Budapest, we exchanged stories of our travels amongst the group – it was by far the most enjoyable train ride I've ever experienced. In fact, once we arrived we continued to hang out with our new friends from the train. I am pleased to say I still maintain friendships with people from that adventure even now.

Walter and I (yes, it was Walter's bottle opener, but I helped) had something that was useful for all the passengers on the train. By sharing what we had, we were not only able to help others, but we benefited from them as well. We saw far more of Budapest than we would have on our own thanks to the guidance and generosity of those we met on the train.

In this journey of life, I have come to appreciate that TCKs and CCKs may have more to offer the world than we probably realize. Don't get me wrong – we're not the answer to all the world's problems. Fixing those is going to take everyone, TCKs and non-TCKs alike. But we do benefit, in many ways, from growing up ahead of our time. *'Ultimately, a cross-cultural childhood is becoming the 'new normal' across our globe for virtually everyone rather than something that only affects globally mobile kids.'*[6] The issues TCKs face are now, and will increasingly be, faced by everyone. TCKs really are a preview of coming attractions.

Technology and global trade have united more of the human race than ever before: more of the global population is onboard the progress train than many could have ever imagined or hoped for. Even if we're on the same train, however, we're often still impeded by our divisions. Whether we're restrictively compartmentalized by nationality or culture or, on a more personal level, by the increased difficulty in maintaining deep and meaningful relationships – this train could do with some liberation.

ALLOPHILIA

I recently learned a term that I think encapsulates a lot of what makes TCKs useful in the world: 'allophilia' – in essence it means the opposite of prejudice. It derives from Greek words meaning 'liking or love of the other.'[7] Another way to see allophelia is as the stage beyond tolerance. Even if it's sometimes learned through the challenging or even painful process of transition, many TCKs learn to move beyond tolerance because of their need to live cross-culturally. Tolerance is a step in the right direction, but it's not the end goal. If you met someone and simply proclaimed you *tolerated* them, nobody would take that as a huge compliment. In some ways, tolerance is a pretty low bar. Moving beyond tolerance doesn't mean going so far as to condone evil, or compromising principles for the sake of peace – far from it. *'For example, when Nelson Mandela was president of South Africa, he attended the 1995 Rugby World Cup finals, cheering for his country's national team – previously regarded as a powerful symbol of 'white' nationalism – and even wearing a team jersey with the captain's number on it. He found within himself a means of embracing aspects of the Afrikaans language and culture – and of encouraging others to do likewise – despite all the injustice and violence that culture had visited upon him and his people. This symbolic act went beyond the mere promotion of tolerance... Mandela seems to have understood the importance of a positive attitude toward the 'other' in bringing about his vision of a multiethnic South Africa.*'[7] For many TCKs, having to move between cultures and learning not only to exist but to thrive in and amongst them means an appreciation for moving beyond tolerance to allophelia.

THE MISSION

Who you are is remarkably valuable. Far from being the culmination of a confusing set of circumstances that are hard to explain, you play a vital role in moving the world forward. Your own experience of growing up in transience or between cultures means you can act as a bridge-builder for a world that is aligning more and more with your reality every day. We are not just an interesting little subculture; we actually offer rare insight into the not-so-distant future. I sincerely hope we will be an encouraging glimpse of things to come: it's a lot to live up to. But if the TCKs I know are anything to go by, I'm not worried. If we, as TCKs and CCKs, can be aware of the challenges we face and consciously act to overcome them, we will be better prepared to use our unique skills to help the world overcome those challenges, too.

So friends: If you ever need to say The Pledge of Allegiance, put your *right* hand on your heart. Enjoy being highly adaptable and be proud to have an identity that surpasses national classifications. Always know where you are before you take your clothes off. Don't underestimate or take for granted what a gift it is to have a broad worldview. Randomly applaud people for entering the room. Look for quality in relationships, not just quantity. Don't ride a horse during a fireworks demonstration. Don't shy away from making the effort to learn how to deal with conflict and not just avoid it: know when it's worth it to stay and put out fires rather than flee them (by way of a terrifying bus or any other means). Strive to always keep an open mind about cutlery use (or lack thereof), fire department organization, and other negotiable aspects of life. Learn the words to a gangster rap song… in a British accent. Trust that the emotional investment required to deal with grief is worth the effort. Prevent unnecessary kidnappings due to being too stuck in the moment to realize you're an idiot who's not listening to your partner-in-crime. Be patient with your parents; don't project your stress onto them (and gently let them know when they project it onto you). Know the truth about budget airlines: what they save you in money they may take from you in sanity. Be welcoming enough to be mistaken for an Internet café and learn to depend on others as they depend on you. Aspire to have reliable transport, and if you ever own a car, name it. Stay cool, liberate a train, and be proud to be a TCK/CCK.

Keep the conversation going

Thanks for coming along on this journey, hopefully you've been able to see some of yourself in my stories – now I'd love to hear your stories too. If you'd like to connect with me, you can do so through Facebook, Twitter, YouTube, Instagram or even good old-fashioned email. I look forward to hearing your adventures!

facebook.com/chrisotalks
twitter.com/chrisosh
youtube.com/lordchristophero
instagram.com/lordchristophero
chris-o@chris-o.com

You can find information about how to book me as a speaker for your school or various other events by visiting www.chris-o.com

Oh yeah, one last list (if you like that sort of thing)...

* Because of moving between cultures and needing to make connections between them, TCKs tend to find it easier to relate and use wider varieties of concepts and information. It's a skill that's widely sought in an ever-globalizing world.

* The world is moving ever closer to the TCK and CCK experience as evidenced by areas such as decreased conflict resolution skills, excess of relationships to deal with, challenges in building community, and the need for more accurate terms for the classification of people.

* Knowing terms like TCK and CCK can help us find a sense of belonging and a way to describe our uniqueness (we need both to be healthy).

* As TCKs and CCKs, we have the potential to be influential bridge-builders as society aligns more and more with our reality and experience everyday. So go, do great things!

[1] *Thomson Reuters Study Proposes Solutions to the Economic Risks of Data Overload.* July 2010 Thompson Reuters.
http://thomsonreuters.com/press-releases/072010/597336

[2] *Strangers At Home.* Carolyn D. Smith. Aletheia Publications. 1996.

[3] http://en.wikipedia.org/wiki/Sonic_hedgehog

[4] *Is Social Media Destroying Real-World Relationships?* 2012. Mashable. http://mashable.com/2012/06/14/social-media-real-world-infographic/

[5] Ted Ward, Sociologist, 1984.

[6] *Belonging Everywhere & Nowhere: Insights into Counseling the Globally Mobile.* Lois J. Bushong, M.S. Mango Tree Intercultural Services. 2013.

[7] *Allophilia – a new framework for understanding effective intergroup leadership.* Todd L. Pittinsky. 2014. http://www.centerforpublicleadership.org/index.php?option=com_content&view=article&id=267:the-allophilia-project&catid=36:cpl-blog

RESOURCES

B At Home, Emma Moves Again. Valérie Besanceney. Summertime. 2014.

Belonging Everywhere & Nowhere: Insights into Counseling the Globally Mobile. Lois J. Bushong, Mango Tree Intercultural Services. 2013.

Bowling Alone: The Collapse and Revival of American Community. Robert D. Putnam. Touchstone Books. 2001.

Burn-Up or Splash Down: Surviving the Culture Shock of Re-Entry. Marion Knell. IVP Books. 2007.

Emotional Resilience and the Expat Child. Julia Simens. Summertime. 2011.

Expat Teens Talk. Dr. Lisa Pittman and Diana Smit. Summertime. 2012

Safe Passage: How mobility affects people and what international schools should do about it. Douglas. W. Ota. Summertime. 2014.

Strangers At Home. Carolyn D. Smith. Aletheia Publications. 1996.

Subtle Differences, Big Faux Pas. Elizabeth Vennekens-Kelly. Summertime. 2012.

The Art of Coming Home. Craig Storti. Intercultural Press Inc. 1997.

The Global Nomad's Guide To University Transition. Tina L. Quick. Summertime. 2010.

The Worlds Within – An anthology of TCK art and writing: young, global and between cultures. Summertime. 2014.

Third Culture Kids, The Experience of Growing Up Among Worlds. David C. Pollock and Ruth E. Van Reken. Nicholas Brealey America; Revised Edition edition. 2009.

A Point of View: Why embracing change is the key to happiness. AL Kennedy. 2013. (Excerpt from *BBC News Magazine*). http://www.bbc.co.uk/news/magazine-23986212

Allophilia – a new framework for understanding effective intergroup leadership. Todd L. Pittinsky. 2014. http://www.centerforpublicleadership.org/index.php?option=com_content&view=article&id=267:the-allophilia-project&catid=36:cpl-blog

Is Social Media Destroying Real-World Relationships? 2012. Mashable. http://mashable.com/2012/06/14/social-media-real-world-infographic/

Teenagers 'only use 800 different words a day'. Aislinn Laing. 2010. (Excerpt from *The Daily* Telegraph). http://mashable.com/2012/06/14/social-media-real-world-infographic/

The Empathy Deficit. David C. Keith O'Brien. 2010. (Excerpt from *The Boston Globe*). http://www.boston.com/bostonglobe/ideas/articles/2010/10/17/the_empathy_deficit/?s_campaign=8315

The 3 'Third Culture Kid' Cultures (http://libbystephens.com/blog/third-culture-kids/31-the-3-qthird-culture-kidq-cultures), Libby Stephens. 2011.

Thomson Reuters Study Proposes Solutions to the Economic Risks of Data Overload. July 2010. Thompson Reuters. http://thomsonreuters.com/press-releases/072010/597336

A Point of View: Why embracing change is the key to happiness. AL Kennedy. 2013. (Excerpt from *BBC News Magazine*). http://www.bbc.co.uk/news/magazine-23986212

What expatriate children never tell their parents. Ellen van Bochaute. http://www.leuvion.com/public/uploads/13106297148700/ExpatKidsEN.pdf

About The Author

Christopher O'Shaughnessy is not only a collector of airline miles, but of adventures. He has the impressive ability to turn life experiences and escapades into captivating tales. His stories entertain and inspire audiences as he explores themes of transition, identity, cross-cultural communication, conflict resolution, and the refashioning of life's challenges into strengths. Christopher has lived in multiple countries and visited nearly a hundred more. He brings this global perspective to both his writing and his speaking.

Christopher has worked with students and young adults for 15 years and is currently a speaker at international schools, community events, service projects, and youth groups around the world. He provides motivational talks, training, workshops, and even graduation speeches and comedy nights. His ability to weave laughter with substance endears him to students, parents and teachers alike. If you are interested in having Christopher speak at your next event or would like to know more about the types of presentations he offers, please email booking@chris-o.com or visit his website: www.chris-o.com.

If you'd like to connect with Christopher through other media you can do so using Facebook, Twitter, YouTube, Instagram or even good old-fashioned email. He looks forward to hearing *your* adventures!

- facebook.com/chrisotalks
- twitter.com/chrisosh
- youtube.com/lordchristophero
- instagram.com/lordchristophero
- chris-o@chris-o.com

Other summertimepublishing books

Expat TEENS TALK

Peers, Parents and Professionals offer support, advice and solutions in response to Expat Life Challenges as shared by Expat Teens

Dr. Lisa Pittman and Diana Smit

The Global Nomad's Guide to UNIVERSITY TRANSITION

Tina L. Quick

THE WORLDS WITHIN

– an anthology of TCK art and writing: young, global and between cultures

Edited by
Eva László-Herbert
and
Jo Parfitt

DOUGLAS W. OTA

SAFE PASSAGE

How mobility affects people &
what international schools
should do about it

"I CANNOT RECOMMEND THIS BOOK HIGHLY ENOUGH"

FOREWORD BY DOUG OTA

EMOTIONAL RESILIENCE
AND THE EXPAT CHILD

Practical tips and storytelling techniques
that will strengthen the global family

Julia Simens

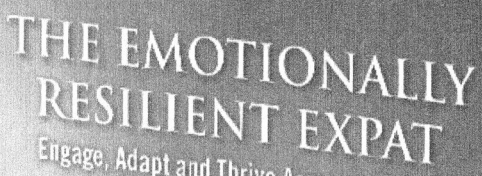

THE EMOTIONALLY RESILIENT EXPAT
Engage, Adapt and Thrive Across Cultures

"Groundbreaking..."
Ruth E. Van Reken
Author of *Third Culture Kids*

LINDA A. JANSSEN

B at Home

Emma Moves Again

By Valérie Besanceney

SUBTLE DIFFERENCES, BIG FAUX PAS
TEST YOUR CULTURAL COMPETENCE

Elizabeth Vennekens-Kelly

Designed by
CREATIONBOOTH
DOT COM

CPSIA information can be obtained at www.ICGtesting.com
Printed in the USA
BVOW06s1233061215

429477BV00008B/148/P